GOD'S THRIFTY EXTRAVAGANCE

GOD'S THRIFTY EXTRAVAGANCE

Understanding What the Bible Says About Money

JONATHAN KOPKE

DISCOVERY HOUSE

PUBLISHERS®

God's Thrifty Extravagance

©2011 by Jonathan Kopke

Discovery House Publishers is affiliated with RBC Ministries, Grand Rapids, Michigan.

Requests for permission to quote from this book should be directed to: Permissions Department, Discovery House Publishers, P.O. Box 3566, Grand Rapids, MI 49501, or contact us by e-mail at permissionsdept@dhp.org

Interior design by Michelle Espinoza

Library of Congress Cataloging-in-Publication Data

Kopke, Jonathan.

God's thrifty extravagance : understanding what the Bible says about money / by Jonathan Kopke.

p. cm.

1. Money—Biblical teaching. 2. Money—Religious aspects—Christianity. I. Title.

BS680.M57K67 2011

220.8'3324--dc22   2010041141

Printed in the United States of America
Second printing in 2011

CONTENTS

One

BURIED TREASURE

The Bible is riddled with paradoxes.

Faith and works.

Grace and truth.

Justice and mercy.

I'm just a Sunday school teacher, so I really don't sit around all day trying to figure out puzzlers like predestination and free will. Quite the opposite, I work as a computer programmer, and we programmers are the people who want every question to have an answer that's true or false, yes or no, 1 or 0, on or off. But some of the most important principles in the Bible just don't work that way, and even those of us who are Bible-believing Christians can find ourselves struggling with paradoxes where two statements from the Bible seem to contradict each other, even while they both ring true.

A while back, an acquaintance of mine named Lucy had to deal with a big example of these ethical tug-of-wars at the orphanage she runs in Kenya. The orphanage gets all of its water from a

spring up in the hills, and one morning the water pipe went dry. Lucy started following the pipeline out of the orphanage and up to its source, and it didn't take her long to find a place where somebody had stolen a few sections of the tubing—probably to sell as scrap. Somehow, the village police caught the culprit right away, and that's when the predicament developed for Lucy. If she didn't press charges, she'd be sending out an open invitation to every pipe pilferer in town—not to mention that the pipe belonged to 150 orphans, and the Bible says that God expects us to "defend the cause of the fatherless" (Isaiah 1:17). On the other hand, God's mercy certainly demanded that a man who stole a few sections of pipe shouldn't be sentenced to a Kenyan prison where he probably wouldn't survive for long. Justice or mercy? Which one should Lucy choose? It was a dilemma posed by two paradoxical scriptural teachings.

There's nothing in the Bible that's more riddled with paradoxes than its relentless discussions of money. Twenty years ago, when I first got involved in a church committee to teach people what the Bible says about our finances, I thought that all we would have to do was look up the Scripture verses about money, write them down, and tell people to obey them. That seemed easy enough—until I ran into a couple of surprises. The first surprise was that the Bible says a whole lot more about money than I had ever realized; the Bible verses about money would make up a one-hundred-page book all by themselves. My second surprise was that any time I found a Bible verse that said something about money, I could usually find another verse that seemed to say the opposite. Paradoxes. Here's one example: Proverbs 10:22 says, "The blessing of the Lord brings wealth, and he adds no trouble to it." But in Matthew 19:23, Jesus says that if we want to know just how much trouble can get added to wealth, all we have to do is take a sewing needle down to the zoo and try a little experiment with the camel. No matter how well we grease the camel, Jesus' little word picture is still going to say that it's all but impossible for someone who's been blessed with wealth to get into heaven. It's a paradox.

Some people deal with these paradoxes by latching on to the side they like best. There are people who latch on to God's mercy, for instance, and they say that the Bible verses about God's justice are just the misguided rantings of some ancient people who weren't as enlightened as we are. Other people latch on to God's justice, and they say that the Bible verses about God's mercy aren't anything we should count on when God is dangling us like spiders over the flames of hell. But neither of those attitudes is really faithful to everything the Bible teaches. And what's worse, as Randy Alcorn says, "Satan is the master of extremes, and he cares little which side of the horse we fall off. He cares only that we don't stay in the saddle." As soon as we favor one side of a biblical paradox over the other, we end up kissing the dirt.

That's probably why a third group of people has tried to deal with the Bible's paradoxes by averaging the two sides of them. But when we try to run ideas like justice and mercy through the blender together, all we end up with is some kind of a gray slop of dithering mercy and weak-kneed justice—and neither of those seems to describe God at all.

So how are we supposed to live in these pickles? Most of the time, we just roll up our windows and hustle past the Bible's paradoxes as if we were driving through the bad part of town. But the approach I want to explore is this: What if we try to savor them? What if we start with the idea that every word of Scripture is "God-breathed" and then try to embrace *both* sides of every biblical paradox?

Where would we end up, for example, if we tried to embrace uncompromising justice *and* immeasurable mercy at the same time? First, we'd have to get past our own stunted understanding of those words. God's justice isn't that petty little get-even impulse that surges up in us every time we get slighted. God's justice is holy. And God's mercy isn't the inconstant little "that's okay" sentiment that gets so tangled up with our own smugness. God's mercy is holy. And if we try to hang on to holy justice and holy mercy at the same time, there's only one place in the world where we can stand upright, and that's at the foot of the cross, where God's holy justice was satisfied and His holy mercy was released.

That's exactly where my friend Lucy was standing when she decided what to do about the man who stole her orphans' water pipes. She pressed charges so that justice would be done. But to make sure that mercy would be worked out too, she told the magistrate that instead of sending the thief to prison, he should order the thief to pay restitution. When the magistrate wondered how Lucy thought a thieving indigent was ever going to pay for the missing pipes, she explained, "I'm hiring him for a job at our orphanage; he'll be our night watchman." "And what does the Lord require of you?" Micah asks, "To act justly *and* to love mercy and to walk humbly with your God" (Micah 6:8).

Going back to the topic of money, where would we end up if we tried to embrace *both* sides of the paradox that says, "The blessing of the Lord brings wealth," and "It is easier for a camel to go through the eye of a needle than for a rich person to enter the Kingdom of God" (Matthew 19:24 NLT)? If we tried to let the Bible explain itself, we might notice first that Ecclesiastes 5:19 reinforces the notion that wealth is a blessing, when Solomon says, "It is a good thing to receive wealth from God and the good health to enjoy it" (NLT). On top of that, we might turn to Genesis 12:2–3, where we would read what God intended when He promised to make Abraham wealthy. God said, "I will bless you; . . . you will be a blessing; . . . and all the peoples of the earth will be blessed through you." If we keep digging, we might eventually come across the verses in Paul's first letter to Timothy that say, "Those who want to be rich fall into temptation and are trapped by many senseless and harmful desires that plunge people into ruin and destruction. For the love of money is a root of all kinds of evil, and in their eagerness to be rich some have wandered away from the faith and pierced themselves with many pains" (1 Timothy 6:9–10 NRSV). John Wesley summed up the situation this way in his sermon "The Use of Money":

> "The love of money," we know, "is the root of all evil," but not the thing itself. The fault does not lie in money, but in them that use it. It may be used ill, and what may not? But it may likewise be used well . . . In the present state of mankind, [money] is an excellent gift of God, answering the noblest ends. In the hands of his children, it is food for the hungry, drink for the thirsty, raiment for the naked. It gives to the traveler and the stranger [a place to] lay his head. By it we may supply the place of a husband to the widow and of a father to the fatherless. We may be a defense for the oppressed, a means of health to the sick, of ease to them that are in pain. [Money] may be as eyes to the blind, as feet to the lame, yea, [as] a lifter up from the gates of death. It is, therefore, of the highest concern that all who fear God [should] know how to employ this valuable talent,

that they be instructed [in] how it may answer these glorious ends and in the highest degree.

So the notions of wealth as a blessing and wealth as a curse are really two sides of the same coin. God blesses us with money—hazardous as the stuff is—so that we can be a blessing. But that blessing comes with a "best if used by" date printed on the label, and when we try to hang on to it too long, it curdles into a blight. Where will we end up if we try to embrace both sides of this paradox about wealth? We and our money will probably end up walking at the edge of hell for the sake of heaven.

There's a lot more to think about in the Bible's paradoxes about money, but before we go on, we need to deal with another little frustration that's bound to come up: Why do there have to be so many paradoxes in the Bible? Why didn't God just explain himself a little more clearly in the first place? And why is it that just about everything the Bible says about money seems to be contradicted by something else the Bible says about money?

The first answer to these questions is that, from God's perspective, there really aren't any paradoxes in the Bible at all. God has never been puzzled by His own justice and mercy, and God has never felt any contradiction between the blessing that money can be and the ghastly influence that money can have.

Yet *we* find paradoxes in the Word of God. Why? Because we're blinded to things that are completely obvious to Him—the same way we're blinded in the old riddle about a mother and her son who were in an airplane crash. The mother was pronounced dead at the scene, but her son was rushed to a hospital. When the life squad rolled the boy into the emergency room, a nurse recognized him right away and screamed, "That's my son!"

Now we have two seemingly contradictory statements: The boy's mother was dead, but the nurse at the hospital yelled, "That's my son!" How could both statements be true? Very simply: The nurse was the boy's father. But in our culture most nurses are women, and when most of us hear this riddle, our cultural preconception about nurses makes it seem as if the two statements are irreconcilable. In fact, they're both completely true and completely consistent.

In the same way, our cultural preconceptions can make two of God's precepts seem contradictory, even when they're both true and perfectly consistent. So we do have problems with biblical paradoxes, but it's not because God himself is conflicted; it's because we have a hard time getting past what's been ingrained in us by our culture, our knowledge, and our prejudices.

All the same, even though there's nothing in the Bible that's puzzling to God, there's plenty that's bewildering to us, and God certainly knew that was going to be the case. So why did God put so many things in the Bible that He knew were going to seem contradictory to us? He did it so often that we would have to conclude that He did it on purpose—but why? Why all these paradoxes?

This is one of those situations where it helps me understand what the Bible *does* say if I think through what the Bible *doesn't* say. Let's imagine for a minute what would happen if the Bible had given us some completely explicit guidelines on how to use our money. What if Jesus had preached, "Truly, truly I say to you, one donkey is enough for the average household. Being a two-donkey family might be okay if the wife works outside the home, but getting a horse wouldn't be anything more than 'keeping up with the Jonases.' And having a camel is simply obscene unless you really have to transport a lot of gold, frankincense, and myrrh"?

First, if the Bible had given us detailed rules like these, they all would have been trapped in one century and one culture. But when the Bible gives us principles that are suspended in dynamic tensions between two ideals, we can apply those principles at any time and in any place.

Second, if the Bible had laid out a whole set of lifestyle rules, I would probably be going around saying, "I am a paragon of Christian money management because I own just one donkey—no horse and no camel." That's legalism, of course, and legalism isn't at all what God is looking for when He gives us His precepts. Someone has said that Jesus didn't come to issue another set of rules, but to propose marriage—and the dynamic tensions of the biblical paradoxes fit into that image of matrimony. Couples don't put a strip of tape down the center of the refrigerator to separate "my" food from "your" food. So too, the Bible's paradoxes about money avoid drawing boundary lines. Instead, they start a dialogue about the values that we gradually learn to share with our Bridegroom in a marriage that will endure "for richer or for poorer."

, Third, if the Bible had laid down detailed lifestyle regulations, and if I saw my neighbors violating those rules, I would judge them. ("Who do those people think they are? Their driveway looks like a used donkey lot.") I would write letters to the editor lambasting them. ("In a world of diminishing resources, no responsible citizen can justify driving a sport-utility camel.") But in contrast to all that condemnation, the dynamic tensions of the biblical paradoxes don't leave me with any basis for judging other people. If I try to denounce people on the grounds of one biblical precept, they can always cite its paradoxical counterpart. Unless I want to be a complete hypocrite, all I can ever claim is that I'm trying to study and pray and grow into a lifestyle that's faithful to both sides of every biblical paradox—and so is every other sincere believer.

Fourth, if the Bible had laid down a lot of absolute financial rules, there wouldn't be much room left for our free will. But when God presents his financial principles in paradoxes instead of laying them down as rules, He gives us wiggle room—just the way He did when He turned Adam and Eve loose in the garden of Eden and said, "Eat anything you want. If you like bananas, they're yours. If you'd rather eat the peaches, have at 'em. Just stay away from that one tree." The financial paradoxes in the Bible give us freedom within constraints. I can drive a secondhand pickup truck, and somebody else can drive a luxury car, and we can both be righteous—as long as we both appreciate that our vehicles are part of how we've been blessed to be a blessing. In the biblical precepts about money, there are a few stay-away-from-that-tree principles, but the paradoxes leave most of the everyday choices up to us.

Finally, if the Bible had laid down specific lifestyle rules, breaking one of those rules would be a sin. But leaning a little too hard toward one side of a paradox doesn't seem like the same kind of offense. When God expresses himself in paradoxes, He's showing us that in most financial decisions, we're not dealing so much with issues of good versus evil as with questions of wisdom versus foolishness. The apostle Paul put it like this: "All things are lawful for me, but not all things are beneficial. All things are lawful for me, but I will not be dominated by anything" (1 Corinthians 6:12 NRSV).

All in all, the truths that God has expressed in paradoxes are buried treasure. They're not hidden *from* us; they're hidden *for* us. "Oh, the depth of the riches of the wisdom and knowledge of God" (Romans 11:33).

I want us to grapple with the five financial issues that trouble Christians the most—owning, saving, borrowing, giving, and spending. As we do, we'll have to work through paradoxes in what the Bible says about every one of these topics. Our goal won't be to pick one side of each paradox and ignore the other. And our goal won't be to split the difference between the two sides of each paradox and try to somehow live out the average. No, our goal will be to figure out how to embrace both sides of each paradox. "It is good that you grasp one thing and also not let go of the other," Solomon says in Ecclesiastes 7:18, "for the one who fears God comes forth with both of them" (NASB).

It isn't easy, this embracing of paradoxes. If God were the invention of human minds—if God were something we had devised to give ourselves a little comfort in an empty universe—then I'm sure we wouldn't have made Him quite so paradoxical. And we certainly wouldn't have invented a Savior who fell asleep in the back of a sinking boat or showed up three days late for a close friend's funeral. But the Bible says that "God's foolishness is wiser than human wisdom, and God's weakness is stronger than human strength" (1 Corinthians 1:25 NRSV). So as we start to explore some of the paradoxes in the Bible about money and possessions, I'm praying a poem that John Donne addressed to Jesus about four hundred years ago:

And through Thy poor birth, where first Thou Glorified'st poverty,

And yet soon after riches didst allow,
By accepting kings' gifts in the Epiphany,
Deliver, and make us to both ways free.

LOOSE CHANGE

Where is Jesus now?

The great missionary and linguist Frank Laubach was troubled by the paradox in the Bible about where Jesus is now. The final paragraph of Matthew has Jesus promising, "Surely I am *with you* always" (28:20) while the last paragraph of Mark says that "[Jesus] was taken up into heaven and he sat *at the right hand of God*" (16:19). Laubach wondered, "How can Jesus be in some far-off heaven and at the same time be with us?" But then he discovered Psalm 139:

You have enclosed me behind and before,
And laid your hand upon me.
If I take the wings of the dawn,
If I dwell in the remotest part of the sea,
Even there Your hand will lead me,
And your right hand will lay hold of me.
(vv. 5, 9–10 NASB)

It suddenly dawned on Frank Laubach that "If, as this psalm says, God's right hand is holding us, and if Jesus is beside God's right hand, then Jesus is close. Where Jesus is, there is heaven, so heaven must be at our elbows. If we knew how to take one step in the right direction, we should be there. God, Jesus, and heaven are that near."

If you can't give me all, give me nothin'—
or something that looks hypocritical

If any Christian sect has an exceptional tolerance for paradoxes, it's the Amish. One good example of that starts with how Amish people see the value of using a telephone for business or for getting help in emergencies, while they also see the danger of using a telephone for gossipy conversations that could undermine their religious community. So in some parts of the country, the Amish bishops have dealt with that tension like this: They won't allow a telephone inside an Amish house where it could be used for tittle-tattle, but they will allow one in an inconvenient "phone shanty" that's out in a barnyard where more than one family has to share it and keep an eye on what it's being used for. To us, that phone shanty may look like hypocrisy, but to the Amish, it looks like a healthy paradox.

Along the same lines, an "Amish tractor" is a gasoline engine that's mounted on a horse-drawn wagon. One Amish farmer joked to Professor Donald Kraybill that "we need the horses to steer it." Kraybill learned, though, that "a tractor is a great labor saver but also a sure way to lose social capital and the joy of collective work." So the Amish will accept a gasoline engine on a horse-drawn wagon, where it can power a hay baler or a grain thresher without wiping out the need for neighborhood work crews that are such an important part of Amish culture.

Some of us could learn a lot from the Amish about living within paradoxes instead of always insisting on taking all-or-nothing stands.

People have teased me about needing lofty principles like this just to decide what salad seasonings to buy, but it really was a liberating moment for me the first time I realized that I could pass up my favorite bleu cheese on one trip to the grocery store as an act of Christ-centered thrift, and then buy it on the next trip as an act of Christ-centered celebration. There *are* times when God presents us with an all-or-nothing ultimatum, but grocery shopping usually isn't one of them. And when we recognize that God not only tolerates paradoxes but also actually seems to favor them, we can be liberated from any sick penchant we have for pointless all-or-nothing rules.

NEGOTIABLES

God's thrifty extravagance

What evidence can we cite from the Bible and from the many revelations of God in nature to support the notion that God practices the Christian virtue of thrift? What evidence can we cite to suggest that God is the most scandalously extravagant individual in the universe? How can we reconcile these paradoxical attributes of God? In our everyday choices, when would it be appropriate for us to practice godly thrift? And when would it be more biblically obedient for us to practice godly extravagance?

Marriage problems for the Bride of Christ

Statistics show that money is one of the two most common causes of problems in marriage. (The other one is sex.) Among people who've been divorced, most say that disagreements about money were a major cause of the failure of their marriage, and the rest say that disagreements about money were *the* cause of the failure of their marriage. The Bible describes the relationship of Christ and His church as a marriage. What disagreements about money are causing problems in this marriage? What can we do to avoid a divorce?

Two

OWNING

PSALM 24:1-2 ~ PSALM 8:1-9

Our heavenly Father has promised to provide for us—just as He provides for the birds of the air. Our challenge is to receive God's providence without behaving like squirrels in the birdfeeder.

If we're asked who really owns everything around us, we all know that the right answer is God, and the Bible certainly teaches that idea. But at the same time, most of the people in the Bible act as if *they* own things, and the Bible seems to accept that idea also, even to the point that the Bible congratulates some people for accumulating lots of money and possessions.

In the Bible, there are two psalms that epitomize this tension between God owning everything and people acting as if *they* owned things. The first one is Psalm 24:

> *The earth is the LORD'S and the*
> *fullness thereof,*
> *the world and those who dwell*
> *therein.*
> *(v. 1 RSV)*

The whole cadence of that verse just rumbles:

Ba boom ba, ba boom ba, ba boom ba, ba BOOM!
The earth is the Lord's and the fullness thereof.

It's a proclamation that has to be thundered to be understood: God owns *everything!*

When we think about God owning the earth "and the fullness thereof," the images that come to my mind are of clouds and mountains, oceans and stars, whales and wildflowers. None of us has any problem with God owning Antarctica and the moon, but this psalm stakes a claim on some things that are a lot closer to home. When Psalm 24 says, "The earth is the Lord's," that would have to include the skyscrapers and the interstate highways and everything else that we think of as "man-made." Even closer to home, "the fullness thereof" would have to include "my" house and "my" car. "My" clothes and "my" food. "My" wallet, "my" checking account, "my" credit card, and "my" tax-sheltered annuity.

Of course, something in me says that *I'm* the one who owns these things—after all, I worked hard to get them. But the Bible comes right back and explains, "You may say to yourself, 'My power and the strength of my hands have produced this wealth for me.' But remember the Lord your God, for it is he who gives you the ability to produce wealth" (Deuteronomy 8:17–19). I can see that the tomatoes in my garden come to me directly from the hand of God. But it's a little harder to see that the rest of what I have comes to me just a little less directly from

God when I trade something else that I got from Him—usually something like strength or skills or time or intellect. As Malcolm Smith puts it, my paycheck might as well read, "To Jonathan, from Father, with love."

But there's more. Psalm 24 insists that it's not just the world that belongs to God; it's "the world and all who live in it." That would include *me*. We belong to God, body and soul. In fact, if we're Christians, we belong to God twice—once because He made us, and once because He bought us back after we had sold out to other influences. "You are not your own," Paul tells us. "You were bought at a price" (1 Corinthians 6:19–20).

It's really hard to grasp just how absolutely God owns the world and everything in it, but the creation story in the Bible has one recurring word that makes God's right of ownership frightfully clear. In the first chapter of Genesis, we read, "God *said*, 'Let there be light'" (v. 3). "God *said*, 'Let the dry ground appear'" (v. 9). "God *said*, 'Let the water teem with living creatures, and let birds fly above the earth across the expanse of the sky'" (v. 20). God somehow *spoke* the entire universe into existence, and it teaches us a lot if we just imagine what would happen if God ever got laryngitis. What would happen if God ever stopped speaking into existence every molecule of the cosmos at every instant? It's not that we'd be blown to smithereens and scattered across interstellar space. It's that there *wouldn't be* any smithereens, and there *wouldn't be* any interstellar space.

"By faith we understand that the universe was formed at God's command," says the author of Hebrews 11:3, "so that what is seen was not made out of what was visible." In the beginning, God created the heavens and the earth *ex nihilo*—out of nothing. And if God ever stopped creating the heavens and the earth for even an instant, they would all revert to nothing. God owns everything because if there were something He didn't own, it would cease to exist. "[Jesus] is before all things," Paul said through inspiration, "and in him, *all things hold together*" (Colossians 1:17). *That* is how absolutely God owns the heavens and the earth.

But that's only half of the Bible's explanation of ownership, and the flip side of the arrangement comes across in Psalm 8. That psalm starts out innocently enough by reaffirming that God owns everything because He created everything—and that we human beings are pitifully insignificant compared to everything else that God has created.

> *O Lord, our Sovereign,*
> *how majestic is your name in all the earth!* . . .
> *When I look at your heavens, the work of your fingers,*
> *the moon and the stars that you have established;*
> *what are human beings that you are mindful of them,*
> *mortals that you care for them?*
> *(vv. 1, 3–4 NRSV)*

So far, there's no tension at all between Psalm 24 and Psalm 8, but one sentence later, Psalm 8 fires a skyrocket in a completely different direction. If I had been the one who spoke the whole universe into being, I would be putting down plastic runners to keep everybody from tracking their dirty shoes all over my creation, but the psalmist says,

> *You have given them dominion over the works of your*
> *   hands;*
> *You have put all things under their feet.*
> *(v. 6 NRSV)*

Inconceivable! God, who has such absolute ownership over everything in the universe, has given us unrestricted dominion over everything He owns. He has put all things under our feet.

This is another idea that's almost impossible to grasp—it's so unimaginable. We know that we can grow crops in God's soil, and we can fish in God's streams. We can drill for God's oil, and we can clear-cut God's timber. We can land on God's moon, and we can split God's atoms—for good or for evil. But there's a lot more to our dominion than that.

One year, right before Christmas, I was in one of those bookstores where a cup of coffee costs as much as a book. The store was swarming with last-minute shoppers, and we were all trying to exercise our dominion over a few more of the works of God's hands in time for the holiday. Whoever ran the store apparently thought that some classical Christmas music might put us in the mood for some classical Christmas spending, so over the top of this whole acquisition panic, the loudspeakers were blaring Handel's *Messiah.* Nobody was really paying any attention to the music, though, and the store's sound system played right past the end of the Christmas part of the oratorio and into the Good Friday section. So while I was elbowing other shoppers out of my way to get to the bargain table, some disembodied soprano right over my head started singing,

> *He gave his back to the smiters,*
> *He gave his back to the smiters,*
> *And his cheeks to them that plucked out the hair.*
> *He hid not his face from shame and spitting.*
> *He hid not his face from shame,*
> *From shame and spitting.*

This, I realized, is the extent of our dominion over all the works of God's hands. We can use God's possessions to dishonor Him. We can turn Jesus' birthday into the high holy day of materialism and spit in His face. We can even drive God's nails into God's cross—through God's hands.

This, then, is the paradox of owning: God has *absolute* ownership over everything in creation, and He has given us *unrestricted* dominion over everything He owns.

I've read that in the original Greek of the New Testament, the word for this arrangement is *oikonomia.* It's used in Ephesians 3:9, where it's usually translated *administration* or *stewardship.* If you squint your ears a little bit when you pronounce the word, you can almost hear that it's the root of our English word *economy. Oikonomia*—economy. But the word *oikonomia* actually comes from two other Greek words: *oikos* (which means "house") and *nomos* (which means "management"). So *oikonomia* is the management of somebody else's house, and a person who does the managing is an *oikonomos*. The Bible teaches that every one of us is an *oikonomos*—a manager, a guardian, a custodian, a trustee, a caretaker—of God's household furniture. "Heaven is my throne," God says, "and the earth is my footstool" (Isaiah 66:1).

Back in the 1600s, when King James put his scholars to work on translating the Bible into English, they scoured the language for a way to capture the whole meaning of *oikonomos* in a single English word, and they discovered that our word *steward* has almost exactly the same history. *Steward* comes from two old Saxon words: *sti* (which means "house") and *ward* (which means "manager"). Back in the seventeenth century, a person who managed a king's estate would have had a title like "The First High Steward of the Royal Household." So the people who translated the King James Version of the Bible settled on the word *steward* as the best translation of *oikonomos*. One place where both forms of the word show up in the same Bible verse is in Luke 16:2 where a rich landowner says to the overseer of his sharecroppers, "Give an account of your stewardship (*oikonomia*), for you can no longer be steward (*oikonomos*)" (NKJV).

In my biggest Bible, stewardship starts on page 1 when God—without ever giving anything to anybody—

says to Adam and Eve, "Be fruitful and multiply, and fill the earth and subdue it; and have dominion over the fish of the sea and over the birds of the air and over every living thing that moves upon the earth" (Genesis 1:28 NRSV). And stewardship is still going strong on page 1,894 when the Bible says, "Like good stewards of the manifold grace of God, serve one another with whatever gift each of you has received" (1 Peter 4:10 NRSV).

It's nothing short of an atrocity that this perfect term *stewardship* has been misused so many times that we usually think it means "fundraising"—as in "The Stewardship Committee will sponsor a fish fry every Friday in Lent." Using the word "stewardship" like this would be enough to make Jesus roll over in His grave—if He were still in His grave. Stewardship isn't a fundraising gimmick; it's a way of life. It's the way of life that just naturally develops when we embrace the paradox that God has absolute ownership over everything in creation while He has also given us unrestricted dominion over everything He owns.

An attitude of stewardship is the foundation for everything else there is to know about a biblical financial lifestyle. Stewardship specialist Eugene Grimm has written that, "Stewardship is what we do after we say, 'I believe.'" And on the flip side of the issue, the fall of humankind can be seen as a failure of stewardship. The problem with Adam and Eve wasn't that they wanted to be like Satan; it was that they wanted to be like God and to live as if they didn't have to answer to Him for how they used His property.

"The earth is the Lord's, and the fullness thereof— the world and they that dwell therein." But the Lord has "given us dominion over all the works of his hands." "Moreover," Paul reminds us, "it is required of stewards that they be found trustworthy" (1 Corinthians 4:2 NRSV).

LOOSE CHANGE

Fundraising for the great ends of the church

In some churches, when the word *stewardship* isn't being used to mean "a manipulative pledge campaign," it's used instead to mean spaghetti suppers, strawberry socials, rummage sales, hog roasts, car washes, bake sales, candy kitchens, carnivals, walk-a-thons, bazaars, corn roasts, and pancake breakfasts. What's worse, some churches think of bingo games, card parties, quilt raffles, and Monte Carlo nights as part of their "stewardship" program. The real problem with these efforts isn't that they're all inherently evil but that they just don't work. If the central task of the church were self-preservation, then a fish fry might serve the purpose. But one time-honored document says in part that "the great ends of the church are the proclamation of the gospel, the nurture of the children of God, the maintenance of divine worship, the preservation of truth, the promotion of social righteousness, and the exhibition of the Kingdom of Heaven to

the world" (The Great Ends of the Church, The Pres-
byterian Church in North America, 1910). And it just
doesn't seem too likely that we're going to accomplish all
of that by going into competition with Red Lobster. It's
more likely that all we're going to do is cheat ourselves
out of the spiritual growth that comes through giving,
and in the process, we'll blur the distinction between the
One Holy Universal Christian Church and the Fraternal
Order of Elks. On top of that, when Philippians 4:19 says,
"My God will meet all your needs according to his glorious riches in Christ Jesus," and when we put up a sign
that says, "Sauerkraut Supper to Benefit the Church," we
might as well put up a sign that says, "God has been a
real disappointment to us when it comes to keeping His
promises."

Administrator of a fortune

If any of us happened to be appointed as the admin-
istrator of somebody else's million-dollar fortune, the first
thing we would do would be to set up some kind of a
ledger book to keep track of the cash. What we don't usually think about, though, is that if we're earning $25,000
a year, over the forty years of a working career, we will be
the administrators of a million-dollar fortune, and that
entire fortune will belong to somebody else, namely God.
How could we dare take on the assignment of managing that much of God's money without some kind of a
budget book?

Most people think of a budget book as a kind of drudgery that's designed to eliminate fun from our lives. But any bookstore offers a half-dozen simple budget workbooks that are designed to focus our money on the things we value most—including fun. In my own household, my wife keeps our budget book on ordinary notebook paper in a three-ring binder. The book gives us a way to make our financial decisions when we're sitting down together at home instead of when we're running through stores separately—and that might explain why we've never once had an argument about money. All we have in our budget book are some very simple pages where we set aside money every month for the most significant things in our life—things like church and food and taxes. When it's time to plan a vacation, for example, and when we get an idea of someplace we'd like to visit, we'll know that our idea is reasonable if it costs less than the amount we've already saved month-by-month in our vacation fund. And while we're on vacation, we won't have to worry about whether we'll be able to pay for the car insurance the next month, because the insurance money is already building up in its own separate fund back home in our budget book. This isn't drudgery; this is liberation.

Unmasking our hearts

In some ways, it's probably easier for us to be good stewards when we don't have much money. If money is tight, and if we're at all sensible, we *have* to spend nearly all of it on things that can't help but be pleasing to God— necessities like food and housing. But when money is more plentiful, then we have choices, and that's when our decisions get a lot more challenging. A study by the Pew Research Center found that "the more income a person has, the more likely he or she is to view goods and gadgets as necessities rather than luxuries." So it's been said that whenever God puts more money under our control, it doesn't really change our hearts—it just unmasks them. Lots of money will do lots of unmasking. There's nothing like a multimillion-dollar building project to unmask the shared heart of a whole congregation.

An un-American virtue

I own an aluminum extension ladder that I use once every fall to put up a couple of storm windows and once every spring to take them down. My neighbor across the street saw that I had the ladder, and he asked if he could borrow it one November to put up some Christmas lights. Of course I let him borrow the ladder, and I told him, "Don't ever buy one of your own; this thing hangs on the wall of my garage 99.99 percent of the time; just help yourself whenever you need it." But the next spring when my neighbor took down his Christmas lights, I saw that he had an aluminum extension ladder of his own. Why? Probably because there's just something un-American about sharing. The American Hero—call him

Daniel Boone or Roy Rogers or Indiana Jones—doesn't go around borrowing ladders. He either has one of his own, or he does without.

On the other hand, while my neighbor and I were squandering the world's known supply of aluminum ore, I happened to be in a Bible-study group with two couples who each had three little boys, and when we got together on Sunday evenings, I noticed that the same little-boy clothes kept getting exchanged back and forth, and back and forth. I suppose I should point out that it was the mothers and not the fathers who seemed to be behind this arrangement. So it was these women's model that I tried to emulate when I wanted a chipper/shredder to take care of our annual mountain of autumn leaves. The cheap leaf shredders looked like toys, and the muscular ones cost a lot more than I could justify for my little yard. But it didn't take me long at all to find three other families from our church who all lived within a block of me and who all wished that they had the high-powered leaf shredder. So we pooled our money, and we bought the five-horsepower monster that could shred a baseball bat. Yes, there are days when we have to wait our turn to use the shredder. And no, nobody but me has ever bothered to change the oil in it. But we've learned that our God is gracious enough to help us share a piece of lawn equipment.

I've known other people who've learned to share labor. ("You help me seal my driveway, and I'll help you paint your kitchen.") And I've read about five families who all sometimes needed more than one car, so they shared a sixth car among them. That group managed to bankroll an entire orphanage in a developing nation with the savings from the four cars they didn't have to buy or maintain. This kind of sharing is so un-American that when we see it in the book of Acts, some people say that the early church was a bunch of socialists.

I once heard a pastor try to define the difference between socialism and Christianity by preaching that, "Socialism says, 'What's yours is mine,' but Christianity says, 'What's mine is yours.'" That would be close to the truth, except that a Christian steward would realize that there's nothing any of us can really call "mine." What happened among the first believers in Acts 4 was that, "The congregation of those who believed were of one heart and soul; and not one of them claimed that anything belonging to him was his own, but all things were common property to them" (v. 32 NASB). So this is my amendment to the preacher's definition: "Socialism says, 'What's yours is mine,' but Christianity says, 'What's God's is ours.'" Our ultimate role model for sharing is of course Jesus, whose entire life was framed between a borrowed manger and a borrowed tomb.

Simplifying simplicity

The lifestyle of Christian stewardship is usually linked with a lifestyle of Christian simplicity. More than once, I've visited a beautiful, Christ-centered community of city people who've been simplifying their lives on a farm just outside of Nashville, Tennessee. One time when I was there, these people told me that they had bought a cow that was pregnant, and the cow had given birth to her calf out in the pasture behind their little meeting house. When the calf was a few weeks old, these people realized that they'd better "fix" it before it grew into a bull they couldn't control. It took them three sultry August evenings of racing around the pasture, flapping their arms, swinging ropes, and jumping out of moving pickup trucks before six men finally managed to grab the calf and pin it on its back. That's when they figured out that the calf was a girl.

Fortunately for the rest of us, Christian simplicity doesn't mean that we have to live like the pioneers. As Richard Foster defines it, simplicity means that we have to focus on a single goal. "*One thing* have I asked of the Lord," David says in Psalm 27:4, "that I may dwell in the house of the Lord all the days of my life, to behold the beauty of the Lord, and to inquire in his temple" (RSV). Kneading whole-grain bread dough might help one person behold the beauty of the Lord—and buying Wonder Bread might be more helpful for somebody else. We need to be careful not to unnecessarily complicate simplicity.

The essence of Christian ethics

Somebody commented to me once about how pious the Muslims are—they pray five times a day. And I'd have to admit that Muslims do trump me in piety if they stop what they're doing five times every day to recite their formal prayers; I don't have that habit. But sometimes I do have to stop five times to pray just while I'm getting into my brown bag lunch at work: "Thank you, Lord, that we have dominion even over microbes so we can make them work for us on turning milk into Colby cheese; it's my favorite, and you provide it for me all the time." Or, "Thank you, Lord, for this big Gala apple; I bought it in the grocery store, but I know it comes from you." Or even, "Thank you, Lord, for caraway seeds in my rye bread; what a nice little touch you added to your universe when you came up with caraway seeds."

When we're always aware of the tensions between God's ownership and our dominion, we seem to keep encountering little caraway seeds that make it almost impossible to forget about God: "Thank you, Lord, that when so many people don't have safe water to drink, I have enough to hose off the driveway." "Thank you, Lord, for the first little hummingbirds of spring. I can put out the nectar feeder, but it's you 'who from zone to zone, guides through the boundless skies [their] certain flight'" ("To a Waterfowl," William Cullen Bryant). "Thank you, Lord, for the good health that makes it possible for me to have a choice about what I'll do today."

A Dutch theologian by the name of G. C. Berkouwer actually decided that "the essence of Christian ethics is gratitude." When we get caught up in this endless conversation with God about all the things He has put under our control, then sinning right in front of Him starts to feel awfully impolite. Charlie Shedd would say that we don't strive to be good stewards so that we can have the love of God forever, but so that the love of God can forever have us.

NEGOTIABLES

Winning a jackpot for God

Once when we were on a vacation to the Grand Canyon, my wife and I flew into the closest city—Las Vegas, Nevada. Before we went, a friend of ours from church told us, "You ought to each take along a roll of quarters and play the slot machines—just till you run out of change. It's exciting. It doesn't cost any more than going to a movie. And if you win a big jackpot, you can give half of the money to the church." We know that (a) all of "our" quarters rightfully belong to God, (b) God has given us complete authority over how to use "our" quarters, (c) there's simply no verse in the Bible that says, "Thou shalt not gamble," and (d) anybody who partied for three days at the wedding reception of Cana can't be all that opposed to other people having a good time. Given what we know about the paradox of owning, what would our biblically informed consciences tell us to do if we had a few rolls of quarters in our pockets and one evening to shoot in Las Vegas?

"The rich get rich, and the poor get poorer"

It's been said that if we took everything that belongs to God and distributed it equally, within six months the rich would be rich again, and the poor would be poor again. Think about people who live as God's stewards, and people who don't. What behaviors of each group would tend to make them end up rich again? What behaviors of each group would tend to make them end up poor again? In general, does good stewardship lead more toward riches or more toward poverty?

Three

SAVING

PROVERBS 6:6-11 ~ LUKE 12:13-21

Anybody who likes some good, hearty put-downs will love the biblical paradox of saving.

"Go to the ant, *you sluggard*," Solomon says, "consider its ways, and be wise! It has no commander, no overseer or ruler, yet it stores its provisions in summer and gathers its food at harvest . . . Poverty will come on you like a bandit and scarcity like an armed man" (Proverbs 6:6–8, 11).

On the other hand, Jesus tells a story about a man who worked just like one of those busy little ants. He stored his provisions in summer and gathered his food at harvest with so much enthusiasm that he had to build bigger barns just to store the surplus. But in the parable, God doesn't congratulate this man on his fine little anthill. No, God says to him, *"You fool!* This very night your life will be demanded from you. Then who will get what you have prepared for yourself?" (Luke 12:20).

So a person who doesn't save is a sluggard, and a person who does save is a fool. You're condemned if you don't—and you're condemned if you do. It's a paradox—and how are we going to embrace both sides of this little conundrum?

As it turns out, this paradox about saving is a lot less troublesome than it looks. To begin with, the Bible is very clear about saying that saving is a good thing. "Precious treasure remains in the house of the wise," Solomon says, "but the fool devours it" (Proverbs 21:20 NRSV). In the book of Genesis, Joseph gets to be a Bible hero by saving enough food during seven years of plenty to last through seven years of famine. And later, when the temple was built in Jerusalem, even it had storerooms where supplies were put aside for the future (1 Chronicles 28:11).

So why did the man who built extra barns get the bum's rush right out of his own parable? His problem was that he *wasn't* saving. He was doing something very different. He was hoarding.

I saw a blatant example of hoarding once when my wife and I were in a wildlife refuge in the Upper Peninsula of Michigan. While we were getting our gear out of the car, I tossed a big square cracker to a flock of birds, and a strapping ring-billed gull snatched it up. A couple hours later, after we had hiked back to our car, I saw the same gull again. I knew it was him because he was still frantically flying around in circles with the whole cracker in his beak. He was so busy keeping his treasure away from the

other birds that he never had a chance to enjoy it himself—or to eat anything else, apparently. Solomon must
have been watching the same kind of behavior when he
wrote, "I have seen a grievous evil under the sun: wealth
hoarded to the harm of its owner" (Ecclesiastes 5:13).

So the ant is wise because he saves, and the seagull
is foolish because he hoards. That's simple enough. But
how are we supposed to know when a nice little stream
of saving is going to back up into a swamp of hoarding?
Here's where we have to live in another dynamic tension,
because the Bible never sets up any flood walls that we
can mark off once and for all with a dollar sign. No, "The
word of God is living and active . . . it judges *the thoughts
and attitudes of the heart*" (Hebrews 4:12). The distinction between saving and hoarding isn't a difference in
magnitude but in motive.

Now, there's certainly nothing wrong with the motive
of wanting to be self-supporting. At one point, the apostle
Paul brags, "We were not idle when we were with you,
nor did we eat anyone's food without paying for it. On
the contrary, we worked night and day, laboring and toil-
ing so that we would not be a burden to any of you"
(2 Thessalonians 3:7–8). And a few verses later, Paul
repeats something that he had apparently told the Thessalonians in person: "If a man will not work, he shall not
eat" (2 Thessalonians 3:10). In a letter to Timothy, Paul
even goes so far as to say that "If anyone does not provide
for his relatives, and especially for his immediate family,

he has denied the faith and is worse than an unbeliever" (1 Timothy 5:8).

The discipline of saving is an integral part of being self-supporting. One time I talked to a real estate agent about his financial problems, and he told me that he felt God had failed him, and he had to depend on money from his elderly mother just to get along. Sometimes, he didn't have enough money to make his own house payments, and sometimes he didn't even have enough to put food on the table for his kids. But when we added up his income for the year, it seemed like it should have been enough. And I really didn't need to have a dream about fat and skinny cows coming out of the Nile to predict that this real estate agent was going to have fat and skinny months in his income, depending on how many houses he happened to sell. So the man's real problem wasn't that God had failed to provide for him. It was just that when God provided a surplus for him during the portly months, he wasn't saving it for the bony months.

For most of us, the importance of saving isn't quite that obvious, but the basic function of saving is still the same. We never know when a bathtub leak is going to sag through the living room ceiling, or the car's transmission is going to get stuck in reverse, or the neighbor's kid is going to launch a bottle rocket into our garage. But what we do know is that, sooner or later, *something* in this blighted world is going to try to get us, and God in His lovingkindness often provides for these hurts before they even happen. Saving is a means of grace—a delivery system for God's goodness. It's the mechanism that God uses most often to provide for life's little emergencies. "Go to the ant, you sluggard. Consider its ways, and be wise!"

But wait just a minute here. I overlooked this for years, but it finally dawned on me that the Bible's image of a hardworking little ant isn't really a picture of self-sufficiency. When an ant "stores his provisions in summer and gathers its food at harvest," he doesn't do it just for himself but for the whole ant community.

If we think about it, we can see that the early church operated a little bit like an ant colony; every member gathered and stored for the benefit of the whole group. Probably the most dramatic example of that is in the second letter to the Corinthians where Paul boasts about how the believers in Macedonia took up a collection to help the believers in Jerusalem. Paul says, "Out of the most severe trial, their overflowing joy and their extreme poverty welled up in rich generosity . . . Entirely on their own, [the Macedonians] urgently pleaded with us for the privilege of sharing in this service to the saints" (2 Corinthians 8:2–4).

On my desk at home, I have a "parallel" Bible that's too heavy to carry around because it gives four different translations of every verse, side by side. And in that parallel Bible, I happened to notice that the New International Version and the King James Version use very different words in that passage where Paul describes what the Macedonians were trying to accomplish with their money. The New International Version says that they wanted "the privilege of *sharing* in this service to the saints," but the King James Version says that they wanted "the *fellowship* of the ministering to the saints." When Paul tells the same story in Romans 15:26, both translations say that the Macedonians were happy just to make a *"contribution"* for the poor among the saints.

I wanted to know exactly what it was that Paul was commending so wholeheartedly about the Macedonians, so I checked these different translations in a dictionary of New Testament words. What I found is that in these verses, *sharing* and *fellowship* and *contribution* are all translations of the same Greek word—and it's a word that's familiar to all of us: *koinonia*.

We usually define *koinonia* with the King James term *fellowship*, but that really risks watering it down to what happens in the "Fellowship Hall"—potluck suppers, mostly. But there's one place in the English language where we still use the word *fellowship* to mean what that word meant back when the King James translators picked it as the equivalent of *koinonia*. When a university gives money to a graduate student to stick around for an extra year of collaborating with other scholars, we say that the student has been awarded a "fellowship." In a very limited way, the student has been awarded a *koinonia*—a chance to be in a partnership where there's sympathetic cooperation and mutual support.

The Greek grammar of this is probably a mess, but when our missionary friends write to us about their prayer needs and their financial needs, maybe instead of saying that they're "raising support" they should say that they're "raising *koinonia*." And instead of saying that we're making a contribution, we could say that we're "making *koinonia*." We're entering into a holy fellowship with another believer and with Almighty God.

So here's the point of all this: The difference between saving and hoarding is a difference in motive, and the motive that distinguishes saving from hoarding is the desire for *koinonia*. "Carry each other's burdens," Paul writes, "and in this way you will fulfill the law of Christ . . . As we have opportunity, let us do good to all people, especially to those who belong to the family of believers" (Galatians 6:2, 10).

About a year ago in our little church, a woman who was dying of cancer couldn't work any longer. She lost her job and along with it her health insurance, and she had to use up every bit of her family's savings just for pain medications. She had come to terms with her own mortality, but she had one last wish: she wanted to be buried wearing her wedding ring. So a week before she died, her husband took what little money they had left, and he got her ring back from a pawnshop. Some of us happened to be washing dishes at the church a few nights later when we got the news that the end had come, and one of our men, just standing there with his hands in the dishwater, started to pray, "Lord, *we* need your help. This funeral is only three days away, and *we* don't know how *we're* going to pay for it."

On the night before the funeral, during the visitation hours at the church, I happened to sit down next to the man who had prayed that way, and he told me, "God's been working, you know." He said, "We got here early to plug in the percolator, and the family was here, but the body had not arrived. So we called the undertaker on his cell phone. Instead of being at *North* Church, he had taken the body to *Northminster* Church. When he got here late with the hearse, he was so sorry about his mistake that he said he'd knock twenty percent off his bill. And that brings it down to what the rest of us said we could put together from our own savings."

This is a blue-ribbon example of righteous saving at work—saving that can't back up into a swamp of hoarding because any excesses will always be drained off through a spillway of *koinonia*. And I wonder if this isn't also an example of at least part of what the Bible promises in 2 Corinthians 9:10, "He who supplies seed to the sower and bread for food will also supply and increase your store of seed and will *enlarge the harvest of your righteousness*."

Saving is what we do when we worry that the hot water heater might fail. Hoarding is what we do when we worry that *God* might fail. Charlie Shedd wrote, "To covet is to believe that God's goodness will run out before it reaches us," and hoarding is an attempt to make sure that can never happen. The main problem with hoarding isn't so much that it's sinful, but that it's stupid. In the Bible, when God condemns the man who built extra barns, he doesn't say, "You sinner!" He says, "You fool!"

A few years ago, a handful of Christian leaders were predicting that the whole American economy was about to go down the drain, and I wondered if I was doing enough to get ready for whenever the stopper might get pulled. I had a chance to talk to a Christian university professor of finance just then, so I asked him for advice. This was a man who was managing a multibillion-dollar mutual fund, so I'm sure he was no enemy of saving. But when I asked him how I should save and what I should save to be safe from "the coming economic earthquake," he just said, "Buy a farm in the most remote location you can find. Buy a lot of seeds. And buy a lot of ammunition." In other words, *no* amount of saving—no amount of gold bullion buried in the basement floor—can ever insulate us from any real disaster. That's a job for God alone. This professor of finance might as well have said to me, "You fool! This very night your life will be demanded from you. Then who will get what you have prepared for yourself?" (Luke 12:20).

The bottom line of this whole discussion is that saving for our future is a wise thing to do, but hoarding without *koinonia* is the height of foolishness. Perhaps this was what John Wesley was thinking about when he preached, "Gain all you can. Save all you can. Give all you can." And that must also be what Saint Ambrose was suggesting when he said, "The proper place to store a surplus is in the mouths of the needy."

If we're ever uncertain about whether we're saving or hoarding, the Christian ideal is to err on the side of *koinonia*, just like Jesus, who "did not consider equality with God something to be grasped [hoarded], but made himself nothing, . . . and became obedient to death—even death on a cross" (Philippians 2:6–8). The worst thing that could happen to us because of that holy recklessness is what Paul describes in Philippians 3:10: We will "know Christ and the power of his resurrection and the fellowship of sharing"—literally, the *koinonia*—"in his sufferings."

LOOSE CHANGE
There's no such thing as a cheap screwdriver

Because saving is a Christian virtue, thrift is a virtue too—but being thrifty isn't the same thing as being cheap. In any bargain store, there are all kinds of tools that look a lot like screwdrivers, but they're really just knuckle-busters or glorified paint can openers. Clearly, it can be better for us in the long run to pay extra for the strength of hardened steel. Along the same line, nothing beats the durability of real wool or the vigor of hybrid seeds.

Similarly, sometimes it's most godly for us to pay more than we have to for an item like gym shoes when we know that the cheaper brand comes from a sweatshop. And here's a more extreme example: When a friend of mine was a kid, his father would give him a nickel if, when he went to the dentist, he would forgo the Novocain. That isn't thrift; that's child abuse. Thrift is a virtue only to the extent that it introduces us, and those around us, to the kingdom of God. Penny-pinching that blocks us or others from the kingdom is an evil from the pit of hell.

When we're living as God's stewards, we don't have to be cheap, and when we're operating according to kingdom principles, we don't have to feel guilty about spending God's money, regardless of the amount. God hasn't suspended us in the dynamic tensions of stewardship in order to make us trudge through every financial decision. Quite the opposite. The writer of Psalm 119:32 says, "I *run* in the path of your commands, for you have set my heart free."

The wisdom from above

We've seen that the distinction between saving and hoarding isn't based on what we do but on why we do it. "For the Lord searches every heart," the writer of 1 Chronicles says, "and understands every motive behind the thoughts" (28:9). God may understand all the motives of our hearts, but it can be awfully hard for us to understand them ourselves. And to complicate the issue, if we're honest, we would have to admit that every time we make a choice, we make it with mixed motives. So when we have to make a decision—financial or otherwise—how can we know with any certainty that we're choosing the

most godly option that's open to us and not just rational-
izing what we would have done even if God hadn't been
around?

In my own experience, I've never heard voices from
heaven telling me exactly what to do. So for me, the sim-
plest approach to making choices is to go ahead and make
a tentative decision on the basis of my own biblically
informed conscience and my own God-given common
sense, and to evaluate that decision against the check-
list that's in James 3:17. That verse says we'll know the
"wisdom from above" when we see it because it's first of
all *pure*. When we've identified the wisdom from above,
we'll notice that our decision-making process has been
peaceable, gentle, and *open to reason*. The outcome of a
godly decision will be *full of mercy* and *good fruits*. And
we won't have to second-guess ourselves later because our
decision will be without *uncertainty* and without *insin-
cerity* (key words from James 3:17 RSV). The greatest
delight that can come out of a decision happens when we
discover that we haven't been trying to justify what we
wanted, but that we've really wanted what *God* wanted
anyway.

NEGOTIABLES

Saving isn't for the birds

In one of the most beloved Bible passages on the providence of God, Jesus says, "Consider the ravens: They do
not sow or reap, they have no storeroom or barn; yet God

feeds them. And how much more valuable are you than birds!" (Luke 12:24). Some Christians teach that, according to this verse, none of us should have a storehouse or barn—in other words, that we should trust God to provide for us the way he provides for the birds and not rely on any savings. If that's not what Jesus means in this passage, what *does* He mean? And how does this verse fit into the biblical paradox of saving?

A bequest for God

A multimillionaire once told me that he had set up a foundation so that every last dime of his fortune would go to Christ-centered ministries—just as soon as he was dead. How does that arrangement hold up in the Bible's tension between saving and hoarding?

Four

BORROWING

We read in the Bible about some really imaginative ways God provides for people. There's a rock in the wilderness that gushes with water. There's a jar of oil that never runs dry. There are ravens that shuttle bread out to a refugee in a ravine. There's a fish that gets caught with a coin in its mouth. There's a little boy's lunch bag that feeds five thousand people. But there is simply no story in the Bible about God providing for somebody through debt. In fact, the Bible bristles with warnings about debt.

Psalm 37:21 sets a foundation for everything else the Bible says about debt. That psalm says, "The wicked borrow and do not repay." So if there's going to be any such thing as biblically acceptable borrowing, this will have to be its minimum standard: Pay back what you've borrowed. Or as Paul puts it, "Let no debt remain outstanding, except the continuing debt to love one another" (Romans 13:8).

But Proverbs 22:7 tightens the clamps a lot more than that. It says, "The rich rules over the poor, and the borrower is the slave of the lender" (NRSV). A slave! And Deuteronomy 28 might have the Bible's all-time most dreadful image of debt. That chapter talks about all the curses of being under a military occupation, and it says, "You will be pledged to be married to a woman, but another will take her and ravish her . . . Your sons and daughters will be given to another nation . . . The alien who lives among you . . . will lend to you, but you will not lend to him" (Deuteronomy 28:30, 32, 43–44). These three things are all listed as parts of the same curse: rape, kidnapping into slavery, and debt.

So far, there's no paradox; the Bible's view of borrowing is uniformly grim. There's no counterpoised principle that favors borrowing, and actually, there's no counterpoised principle at all—unless we can count that there's an awfully loud silence in what the Bible *doesn't* say about debt. The one verse that we would most expect to find in the Bible never actually shows up. "Neither a borrower nor a lender be" is from *Hamlet*—not Hosea. And in fact, the Bible even hints a few times that "Thou shalt not borrow" wasn't left out of the Ten Commandments by accident.

The psalmist says, "Good will come to him who is generous and lends freely" (112:5). And in Matthew 5:42, Jesus himself says, "Give to the one who asks you, and do not turn away from the one who wants to borrow from you." Now, these verses are obviously talking about a lot more than money, but the point remains that if lending can be so commendable, then borrowing can't be entirely unthinkable.

So this is the paradox of borrowing: over and over again, the Bible speaks very harshly about debt, but the Bible never actually bans debt. And just how are we supposed to embrace both sides of this puzzler? By going into debt just a little bit?

Here again, though, it turns out that if we just let the Bible explain the Bible, the difference between bondage-debt and okay-debt isn't all that complicated. If we read the Bible carefully, we can see that it never really condemns debt itself. What it condemns are two other evils that are so tangled up with debt that we usually can't separate them. But if we *could* figure out how to separate them, some kinds of debt might turn out to be okay.

Nehemiah 5:10 is one passage where the first poison of debt shows up clearly. In that passage, the prophet is scolding some of his countrymen, and he shouts, "I and my brothers and my men are also lending the people money and grain. *But let the exacting of usury stop!*" It's obvious here that Nehemiah isn't condemning people for making loans; he's been doing the same thing himself. But Nehemiah is condemning some of his countrymen for "exacting usury."

Usury is an old-fashioned English word that means "an exorbitant or unconscionable rate of interest." But Eugene Peterson gets to the real essence of usury more simply when he paraphrases Nehemiah 5:10 to say, "I and my brothers and the people working for me have also loaned them money. But this *gouging them with interest* has to stop" (*The Message*).

In our culture, nobody studies the word *usury* anymore, but some scoundrels have really gone to the head of the class when it comes to gouging people with interest—and the rest of us just seem to accept it. We're so accustomed to usury that we're not even scandalized when a credit card company charges us 21 percent interest. And we act as if zero percent financing on a new car is a spectacularly good rate of interest, when actually, we can't get the zero percent financing unless we pass up a couple thousand dollars in "cash back"—hidden finance charges.

God, on the other hand, is outraged when people get gouged with interest, especially when the people getting gouged are the poor. In the book of Ezekiel, God lists about nine things that would make Him angry enough to annihilate somebody, and three of them are, "He oppresses the poor and needy . . . He does not return what he took in pledge . . . He lends at usury and takes excessive interest" (18:12–13). When a "payroll advance" shop charges the down-and-out something like fifteen dollars for a two-week loan of a hundred bucks, or when an income tax service in an inner-city neighborhood does the same thing and calls it an "instant refund," that's actually the same as charging an annual interest rate of

390 percent. Elijah called bears out of the woods to eat people for doing things that weren't *that* bad. There are very few financial sins named in the Bible, but exacting usury is one of them.

Of course, most of us don't have to worry about ever being guilty of exacting usury; even if we wanted to, we'd never be in a position to do it. On the other hand, most of us are vulnerable to becoming the *victims* of usury. And even though being a victim isn't a sin, the bondage of usury doesn't seem like something we should be volunteering for. "It is for freedom that Christ has set us free," Paul says in Galatians 5:1. "Stand firm, then, and do not let yourselves be burdened again by a yoke of slavery."

So usury is one poison that's almost always tangled up with debt, but there's another. James writes, "Now listen, you who say, 'Today or tomorrow we will go to this or that city, spend a year there, carry on business and make money.' Why, you do not even know what will happen tomorrow" (4:13). If we defy this truth and borrow money as if we *did* know what will happen tomorrow, then we're opening ourselves up to another whole world of bondage.

Suppose I get a new car loan, and then suppose that the "Don't Know What Will Happen Tomorrow" happens tomorrow. Say I get downsized out of my job, or Grandma goes into a nursing home and racks up such tremendous bills that I can't afford my car payments anymore. It would really help if I could just take the car back to the dealer and trade down to a cheaper one, but I can't do that because as soon as I drove the car off the dealer's lot, it turned into a used car, and it isn't worth as much as I still owe on it. People in the credit industry call this being "upside down" (or "underwater") in debt. Once I'm upside down, I might have to pay thousands of dollars just to get the dealer to take the car off my hands. The problem will have started because I promised to pay a debt when I really didn't know if I'd be able to keep my promise. Some Christians call this "presuming on the future." And if some people think that the outcome of it doesn't sound like a form of bondage, just let them try missing a few car payments to see what happens. Early eighteenth-century Bible scholar Matthew Henry wrote, "Christians must be careful not to contract any debts they have not the power to discharge. They are also to stand aloof from all venturesome speculations and rash engagements, and whatever may expose them to the danger of not rendering to all their due."

Now, where does all this information about debt leave us? If debt isn't intrinsically evil, but it is bondage to get trapped in excessive rates of interest, and it is bondage to get trapped in promises that we can't keep, then is there any such thing as biblically obedient borrowing? The answer is yes, and it's interesting to me that modern lawyers have a special name for the one kind of loan that meets the Bible's standards. They call it an "exculpatory loan."

I'm not going to pretend to know anything about Latin, but the word *exculpatory* practically falls apart in my hand. *Ex* means "out of"—as in our word *exit*. And *culpa* means "guilt"—as in our word *culpable*. So an exculpatory loan is one that gives me a way of staying out of guilt. An exculpatory loan (sometimes called a nonrecourse loan) satisfies all of the biblical ideals for borrowing and lending. There's a catch, of course. Even though there are such things as these stay-out-of-guilt loans, they're very rare, and there's really only one field where they're used much at all: exculpatory home loans.

We usually use the terms *mortgage* and *home loan* as if they meant the same thing, but they're actually two separate agreements. When my wife and I went to the bank for the "closing" to buy our house, one of the papers we had to sign was the home loan. That's where the bank gave us lots of money to pay for the house. But another paper that we signed was the mortgage. That's where we turned the house over to the bank as collateral until we could pay back the loan.

In a truly exculpatory home loan (and in recent history, most home loans have *not* been exculpatory), the mortgage on the house is what backs up the debt. The bankers agree in advance that if I get downsized out of my job or if Grandma goes into a nursing home and racks up such tremendous bills that I can't afford my house payments, the bank will take the house back and call it even. Now, that's certainly not the outcome anybody wants, including the bankers. But the important point here is that if the interest on a home loan isn't excessive, and if it isn't rigged to become excessive in a few years, then the mortgage arrangement can be biblically solid. It's a borrowing plan that's designed to keep us out of bondage even though we "don't even know what will happen tomorrow."

There might be a few other uncommon forms of debt that would meet all of the Bible's standards, but in general, a biblically obedient person would want to avoid nearly all debt, except perhaps for an exculpatory home loan. And even in that case, there's something to be learned from the fact that, until the housing boom after World War II, most home loans were for only seven years, and having a mortgage was something that people didn't want their neighbors to know about.

Once again, the paradox of borrowing is that the Bible uses uncommonly harsh language to warn us that debt is hazardous, and at the same time, it cautiously hints that there's nothing innately evil about making use of the few forms of debt that manage to avoid its worst hazards.

There's one more important facet to this paradox though. I read a story about a soup kitchen where the patrons had to sit through a sermon before they got their supper. One night, the preacher tried to inspire all of the old drifters by reciting that famous graduation-card poem called "If" by Rudyard Kipling:

"If you can wait and not be tired by waiting . . ."

"If you can dream and not make dreams your master . . ."

"If you can talk with crowds and keep your virtue . . ."

And the preacher went on and on with Kipling's "if this" and "if that" until finally one old guy in the back of the hall stood up and groused, "And what if you can't?"

What if you can't? What if you just can't avoid the kinds of debt that the Bible condemns so sternly?

I knew a couple who had to take their teenage son to a specialist, and the doctor decided that the young man needed surgery to reconstruct his jaw or he would be in pain for the rest of his life. But this couple's health insurance company ruled that the surgery was "cosmetic" and wouldn't cover it. Maybe this family could have done a better job with the virtue of saving beforehand, but they simply didn't have twenty thousand dollars on hand for an operation. They wanted to follow the Bible's precepts and stay out of debt, but they couldn't. "And what if you can't?"

This kind of situation makes us grateful for the clemency that keeps showing up in all of the Bible's paradoxes about money and possessions. This paradox of borrowing doesn't force us to make some kind of a choice between good and evil. It just suspends us in a tension between caution and permission. Nothing in the Bible says it's a sin to take out a loan for a son's operation—and in fact, it might be a sin not to. The desperation my friends felt about their son's health didn't make their borrowing any less risky; it just made it necessary. And the Bible doesn't say that desperate borrowing is evil, but it does warn (strongly and repeatedly) that desperate borrowing should be our last resort.

The Bible's precepts about borrowing don't set up a penal code; they issue an emancipation proclamation. God hasn't made up a book of arbitrary rules to keep us from having any fun. But when it comes to borrowing, He's lovingly suspended us in a set of dynamic tensions that give us one more way of experiencing and preserving what Romans 8:21 calls "the glorious freedom of the children of God."

LOOSE CHANGE

Appreciating our depreciating assets

Some people have taught that a loan to buy a *depreciating* asset is a bad loan, while a loan to buy an *appreciating* asset is a good loan. It's true that we tend to get "upside down" in car loans because cars *depreciate* so quickly when they're new. And it's also true that we tend to *not* get upside down in home loans because (at least in normal economic times) houses generally *appreciate* while we own them. But that's not what makes a home loan more biblically sound than a car loan. What makes a home loan relatively acceptable is the fact that it is fully *collateralized*. Naturally, lenders are a lot more inclined to accept an appreciating asset as collateral, but an exculpatory home loan doesn't keep us out of bondage only if the value of our house goes up. It keeps us out of bondage even if the value of our house goes down. That's also why we need to read the paperwork before we sign our names; not all home loans are exculpatory loans.

Blessing by withholding

We all know that sometimes parents can bless their children by not letting them have a car, or by not letting them go to Florida for spring break with their friends, or even by not letting them spend their own money stupidly. But we hardly ever stop to think that our heavenly Parent can bless *us* by withholding. One of the most dangerous aspects of easy credit is that it can help us get something when God has been blessing us by withholding it.

Save now, and buy later

According to Internal Revenue Service statistics, the typical American family devotes ten times as much money to interest payments as to charitable contributions. What would happen if we could all just reverse our "buy now, and pay later" strategy into "save now, and buy later"? For starters, we would have interest working for us instead of against us. And we could, in effect, give ourselves a huge raise. But beyond that, we could devote a whole lot more of our resources to kingdom purposes—and we could do it *with no change at all in our lifestyles.*

A few weeks away from bankruptcy

On TV, I see a man in a plaid suit shrieking, "I don't care about making money; I just *love* to sell carpet." He always promises, "No payments until March five years from now"—by which time the finance charges will have added up to a lot more than the price of a rug.

At the entrances to the biggest stores in our shopping malls, I often see people handing out coffee mugs and bobblehead dolls and 10 percent discount coupons to anybody who'll sign up for their store's credit card—but those people never seem to mention that most of those big stores actually make more money on finance charges than they do on merchandise.

Just about every day in the mail I get a couple more offers for credit cards with twenty-five thousand free frequent-flyer miles—which just exposes the fact that the credit card companies expect to make a lot more money from my finance charges than what they'll have to pay for my so-called "free" airplane ride.

Is it any wonder that the typical American family is a few weeks away from bankruptcy—totally dependent on next month's income to pay last month's bills? Larry Burkett used to point out that "No young couple has ever said, 'Let's get married, sink hopelessly into debt, fight about money, and then get divorced'—but that's exactly what half of the couples in America do." If we're going to get any benefit from what the Bible teaches about borrowing and lending, we're going to have to do a much better job of exposing what the commercials and the discounts and the junk mail are really offering: free lies.

What about lending?

We've seen that the Bible sets up some narrow guidelines for borrowing, but what about lending, and especially, what about lending at interest?

In Exodus 22:25, Moses says, "If you lend money to my people, to the poor among you, you shall not deal with them as a creditor; *you shall not exact interest from them*" (NRSV). There are several other Old Testament passages that say essentially the same thing, and Leviticus 25:35, 37 is one of the clearest examples: "If one of your countrymen becomes poor and is unable to support himself among you, . . . *you must not lend him money at interest.*"

Because of Bible verses such as these, the Christian church taught for well over a thousand years that, "You can lend, but you can't charge interest," and even today, some factions of the Christian church still teach that the capitalist system has to go. These teachings have never put the moneylenders out of business, of course. They've just put the moneylenders out of the church.

But we can see—and church scholars since the Middle Ages have gradually realized—that these Old Testament passages about interest always seem to lead off with the words, "When you lend to the poor . . . " So the real issue in these verses isn't interest; it's our attitude toward the poor. In his first letter, John says, "If anyone has material possessions and sees his brother [or sister] in need but has no pity . . . , how can the love of God be in him?" (3:17). So how much worse is a person who has the world's goods, and sees brothers and sisters in need, and tries to exploit them by trapping them in interest payments while they don't have any other options! The Bible makes it perfectly clear that it's wrong to do that. But while the Bible never explicitly endorses the idea of lending at interest *without* exploiting people, it does seem to leave that possibility open for discussion.

So now let's say that we're in a position to lend money— not to people who are desperate to buy groceries but to people who are ambitious to buy a grocery store. There's nothing in the Bible to suggest that this kind of loan would be intrinsically evil, but even so, we'll need to take some precautions to make sure that it can't go bad.

First, we'll need to have a plan in place for what we'll do if the grocery business fails. If that happens, and we demand all of our money back, plus all of the interest that we ever expected to collect, we'll be right back in the position of exploiting people who haven't been as blessed as we are. So from the start, we'll need to build into our loan some kind of an emergency escape hatch that's fair for everybody—just the way bankers have the option of using a mortgage as an escape hatch for a failed home loan.

Second, we'll need to make sure that we're not charging an exploitative rate of interest on our loan. As far back as the thirteenth century, church scholars understood that any time we invest money in one place, we give up the profits that we could have earned by investing it in some other place. So it's not inherently exploitative for us to expect to make up for our loss by collecting a reasonable fraction of the profits of our borrowers, and in fact, if we didn't collect any interest from them, they'd be exploiting *us*. But when we set the interest rate on a loan, we'll need to make sure that it isn't out of line with the borrower's anticipated profits or the income we could have reasonably expected from using our money in some other way. In other words, we'll need to make sure that we're not exacting usury.

Put these two safeguards together, and *voilà*—we've just invented the lender's side of an exculpatory loan. Any discussion that's this short is going to be inadequate, but basically, these are the constraints on biblically obedient lending. John Wesley wrote that we should never try to exact interest from someone who has "borrowed for necessity" and over whom we have an advantage. And we should restrict ourselves to lending only in circumstances where we share "in loss as well as in profit." But in those limited circumstances, Wesley said, "It seems as lawful to receive interest for my money as it is to receive rent for my land."

NEGOTIABLES

Borrowing your own money

Some friends of mine had a daughter who turned out to be so talented at playing the cello that it didn't take her long to reach a point where she was stymied by her school-orchestra instrument. Of course her parents wanted the girl to keep developing her talents, but they didn't have ten thousand dollars lying around to pay for a first-rate cello. After a lot of deliberation, the family decided to borrow the money for a new cello from the father's retirement plan. If he had died or become disabled while the loan was outstanding, it would have been deducted from his benefits. The interest he had to pay on the loan was about the same as the dividends the money would have earned while his pension plan had it invested for him. Cite some specific principles from the Bible to evaluate how this loan stacks up against God's guidelines for borrowing.

Cosigning a loan to buy a slippery slope

Many teenagers ask their parents to cosign a car loan or a student loan. If we had this opportunity to influence an individual at the beginning of adulthood, how could we explain the biblical principles that are at stake? What should be our response to the actual request to cosign the loan? What mitigating circumstances, if any, might make us reverse our decision?

Five

GIVING

What do you get for the God who has everything?

God doesn't exactly need another necktie, after all. And for that matter, in Psalm 50, God is pretty blunt about saying that He doesn't really need anything from us at all. He says, "I have no need of a bull from your stall or of goats from your pens, for every animal of the forest is mine, and the cattle on a thousand hills . . . If I were hungry I would not tell you, for the world is mine, and all that is in it" (vv. 9–10, 12).

But several hundred pages later, in Malachi, the same God turns right around and says, "Will anyone rob God? . . . Bring the full tithe into the storehouse, so that there may be food in my house" (3:8, 10 NRSV).

So here we go again with another paradox. God says that if He were hungry, He wouldn't even bother to tell us, but He also says that we're robbing Him if we don't keep His storehouse stocked with food. And just how are we supposed to

71

embrace both of these grocery images when they seem so completely contradictory?

I used to think that we could resolve this paradox by saying that even though God doesn't really *need* our help, He *wants* our help. He lives in the kingdom of heaven, and He wants us to take charge of building that kingdom here on earth. Fortunately, after I had been teaching that "heresy" for a few years, I happened to overhear our pastor explaining to somebody that in the Bible, God never asks any of us to build His kingdom. I've looked it up, and I discovered that in the Bible there are some people who *wait* for the kingdom, and Jesus tells all of us to *seek* the kingdom. The kingdom can *come*, and it can *appear*. The kingdom can *be conferred* on us, *given* to us, and *handed over* to us. We can *preach*, we can *declare*, and we can *proclaim* the kingdom. We can *see* the kingdom, we can *enter* it, we can *take our places in* it, we can *lay hold* of it, and we can *inherit* it. But nowhere in the Bible does God invite us—let alone command us—to *build* His kingdom. And as I think about it now, it was awfully presumptuous of me to assume that the kingdom of God would come with some assembly required.

So "building the kingdom of God on earth" doesn't work as an explanation for why God demands so much out of us when He doesn't need a single thing from us. But before we can get to the real crux of this paradox, we have to take a detour for a minute and think about the spiritual power that money exerts on us.

Somewhere in my house I have about a dozen silver dollars that my grandfather gave me when I was a little kid. None of those coins is really worth a whole lot, but Grandpa gave them to me, so I've held on to them. I keep those silver dollars hidden in an old, hollowed-out book somewhere, and it's been so many years since I've even looked at them that I'm not really sure where that book is right now. But through all the decades that those silver dollars have been sitting there in the dark without anybody even touching them, their value has kept going up and down and up some more, probably every day. There's something about that money that's almost alive.

Now, I'm not saying that all money is demon-possessed or anything like that, but money is somehow alive, and money exerts a spiritual force on us. There aren't very many of those silver dollars in my hollowed-out book, so they don't seem to be able to bark orders at me very loudly. But in other places where I have more money tucked away, there's a constant yapping. Money is always trying to tell us what to do. And if we want to be honest with ourselves, we'd have to admit that on some of the most important occasions of our lives, we've already done exactly what money told us to do.

For one example, how did my wife and I choose the house we live in? Did we go to a real estate agent and say, "Here's a list of our Christian convictions; help us find a house that'll make it easier for us to live them out"? Of course not. We went to a real estate agent, and we said,

"Here's how much money we make." And with very little information other than that, the agent found a house that seemed right for us. So who actually made the biggest financial decision of our lives? In a very real way, the money itself did.

If money didn't do anything but tell us what to buy, that would be troublesome enough, but money skulks its way into all kinds of decisions that are a lot more significant than that. I remember sitting in my high school guidance counselor's office the afternoon money decided where I would go to college. About ten years later, I chose my career as a computer programmer mostly because that's the job where a person with my aptitudes can make the most money. And now I'm at the stage of life where tens of thousands of dollars in "retirement incentives" are trying to tell me that it's time to stop pushing a mouse around all day and go home.

It gets worse than that, though. Money must have an awfully big role in screening my friends—either that or it's an incredible coincidence that almost all of my friends earn just about the same amount of money as I do. And money even shapes my self-image. I can feel good about myself because I'm one of the most highly paid people in my work group. Or I can feel bad about myself because I don't make as much money as my brothers-in-law.

Money is always barking orders: Buy this! Choose that! Feel a different way! One of my friends at work told me that his wife hadn't baked a cookie in a decade, but when they remodeled their kitchen, she had to have not one, but two built-in ovens. Who made that decision? I think it was a home equity loan.

Money doesn't always tell us to buy things we don't need; sometimes it can tell us *not* to buy things we *do* need. A few years back, I teamed up with a friend of mine from church to visit Bible-study groups to talk about money. My friend would tell how, when he was in his twenties, he liked to carry five thousand dollars in his sock, just in case his fantastic income made him want something. Then I would tell how, when I was in *my* twenties, I walked around college with freezing rain dripping off my hair all winter because my money wouldn't let me have something so frivolous as an umbrella. The point my friend and I were trying to make was not that between the two of us we had lived a balanced life, but that both of us had been driving under the influence of money.

Money exerts such a powerful influence on us that some translations of Matthew 6:24, including the New International Version, put a capital "M" on the word when Jesus says, "You cannot serve both God and Money." In some of the older translations of the Bible, that word *Money* is rendered as *Mammon*, but in either case, the message is the same. Jesus is using the words *Money* or *Mammon* as the name of a rival god. And Jesus doesn't say, "*Don't* serve God and Money." He says, "You *can't* serve God and Money." It's impossible. The orders from the one are never going to line up with the commandments of the other.

In the book of Joshua, the writer tells us that when more than one god tries to influence us, we have to make a decision. "If serving the Lord seems undesirable to you," Joshua says, "then choose for yourselves this day whom you *will* serve" (24:15). But you can't have it both ways.

Assuming that we *do* want to serve the Lord, how can we squelch the rival god of Money? How can we stop Money from making all of our decisions for us? In 1 Timothy 6:17–19, Paul describes this plan: "Command those who are rich . . . to do good, to be rich in good deeds, and to be generous and willing to share. In this way, they will lay up treasure for themselves as a firm foundation for the coming age, so that they may take hold of the life that is truly life." In other words, we can start to break the power that Money lords over us, and we can start to "take hold of the life that is truly life," by simply giving Money away.

This certainly isn't the only reason for giving. And it may not even be the *best* reason for giving. But it's a *sufficient* reason for giving, and it's the reason that resolves the biblical paradox about giving. If God doesn't need a single thing from us, why is He so adamant that we should give Him so much? The answer is simple: God wants us to give to Him because that's what breaks us free from the tyrant-god of Money. Giving to God reduces our attachment to the things we've loved more. Giving to God builds our commitment to Him by putting our treasure where we want our hearts to be. Giving to God strengthens our *koinonia* within the body of Christ, the church. Giving to God—as opposed to hoarding—is the most concrete way we have of expressing our faith in the God who promises that He'll never fail us. And in every case, when we give to God, it's not God who benefits—it's us. God doesn't want our gifts because He needs to receive, but because we need to give.

Of course, that leads to another problem. I don't want to sound disrespectful here, but let's face it: receiving is one of those things God simply can't do. We've seen Psalm 50, where God says, "Every animal of the forest is [already] mine, and the cattle on a thousand hills" (v. 10). In Haggai 2:8, God says, "The silver is [already] mine, and the gold is [already] mine." In Leviticus 25:23, God says, "The land is [already] mine." And in Exodus 19:5, there's another of those verses in which God just comes right out and says, "The whole earth is [already] mine." So how can we possibly give anything to God when He already owns everything there is?

Well, God is certainly aware of that little dilemma, and He's so enormously kind that He has come up with another simple mechanism to get us past it. "Truly I tell you," Jesus explains in Matthew 25:40, "just as you did it to one of the least of these who are members of my family, *you did it to me*" (NRSV).

God knows how critically we need to give to Him, but He also knows just how impossible it would be for us to actually do that. So He's appointed some people to stand in for Him as His official receivers. Frankly, they're an unlikely bunch to be standing in for God. Some of them might be out sleeping under a freeway bridge right now. Some of them might still be growing in the wombs of rebellious teenagers. Some of them are undoubtedly people living in undeveloped countries—people who not only don't have a Bible in their own language but who also don't even have an alphabet in their own language. And some of these surrogate receivers must be the pastors and the nurses and the missionaries who are delivering our gifts to God by delivering them to "the least of these, the members of God's family."

But when the Bible says that "God loves a cheerful giver" (2 Corinthians 9:7), it doesn't stipulate anything about being a cheerful giver only to officially registered 501(c)(3) organizations where our contributions will be deductible for federal income tax purposes. No, God loves the person who gives cheerfully to "the least of these" in any circumstances. In our church, a woman who has bone problems finally got a new job on an assembly line after she'd been out of work for a long time. She told me that another woman in the congregation had paid for her to have a pair of orthopedic shoes custom-made so she could literally get back on her feet.

When my wife had to go through chemotherapy, some of the other ladies in our church took her shopping for a wig, and they added their own money on top of what our insurance would pay so my wife could have a more natural-looking hairpiece. And I know one man who's been an extraordinarily big tipper ever since he realized that leaving a tip is an easy way to give to one of "the least of these, the members of God's family." Jesus says that all of this giving counts. It counts as giving to Him, and it counts for eternity.

Naturally, when we realize that learning to give is a big part of breaking loose from the influence of money and submitting to the influence of God, that raises one more question: How much of our money do we have to give away in order to teach the rest of our money a lesson? The Bible's guidance on this question starts with the idea of a tithe.

Tithe is an Old English word that means "a tenth," and the verb *to tithe* means "to give a tenth" of our income to God. Well, actually, that's not completely accurate because we don't have anything that we could properly call "our" income, and even if we did, we wouldn't be able to give it directly to God. So it would be better for us to define *tithing* more like this: "To tithe is to set aside for God a tenth of what He's entrusted to us." And in God's economy, giving ten percent seems to be just far enough out of our comfort zone that it's a tipping point for our spiritual growth.

In our country, tithing isn't very common, even among devout Christians, and most of us have a lot of misconceptions about it. In fact, in both the Old Testament and the New Testament, tithing is simultaneously *much more* and *much less* than most of us have probably ever imagined.

First, tithing in the Old Testament is a lot *more* than we probably ever imagined. In the Old Testament, there are actually several tithes. We seldom read these parts of the Bible, but Numbers 18 mentions an annual tithe that went to the religious establishment. Near the end of Deuteronomy 14, Moses mentions a second tithe that was supposed to finance some religious festivals. And in the last few sentences of the same chapter, he mentions one more tithe that was collected only every third year, and it was for taking care of widows and orphans. To be completely honest about this, some Bible scholars think that the second and third tithes may have overlapped, but the fact remains that tithing in the Old Testament was never just ten percent. It was at least twenty percent every year, and in some years, it was probably more like thirty. Tithing in the Old Testament is a lot more than we usually think.

At the same time, the "law of tithing" in the Old Testament may be a lot *less* than we usually think. When people break a law, we expect them to be punished, and Old Testament laws have punishments built right into them. For example, in the Old Testament, there's a law that says, "If someone strikes and kills another person . . . it is murder, and the murderer must be executed" (Numbers 35:16 NLT). But in all of the Bible, even though tithing is prescribed in quite a few different places, there's never a direct punishment listed for a person who fails to tithe. This seems to imply that tithing was never really much of a law, and so in at least this one sense, tithing in the Old Testament is a lot *less* than we usually think.

Not so surprisingly, tithing in the New Testament is also *less* than some people have claimed. Galatians 5:18 says, "If you are led by the Spirit, you are not under the law." So even if tithing had been a strict Old Testament law, it wouldn't apply to us. We're "led by the Spirit"; we're not subject to Old Testament laws. We don't hold to Sabbath/Saturday regulations, we don't pass up the pork chops, and we're not required to tithe. Tithing for New Testament Christians is a lot *less* than some people have taught.

On the other hand, tithing in the New Testament is *much more* than we usually assume. In Matthew 23:23, Jesus scolds the religious leaders: "Woe to you, teachers of the law and Pharisees, you hypocrites! You give a tenth of your spices—mint, dill and cummin. But you have neglected the more important matters of the law—justice, mercy and faithfulness." It's as if they were being told, "You bunch of phonies! You're going through your spice cabinets, and you're spooning out for God exactly one tenth of what's in every little jar, but you're not paying any attention to the things that are really important to God—justice, mercy, and faithfulness."

Does Jesus mean that we should forget about tithing and concentrate on the more important things? Apparently not. Just look at the very next sentence that comes out of His mouth: "You should have practiced the latter [justice, mercy, and faithfulness], *without neglecting the former* [meticulous tithing]" (Matthew 23:23). Jesus isn't telling the Pharisees that they've been doing too much by tithing so scrupulously; He's telling them that they've been doing too little. Earlier, in Matthew 5:20, Jesus warns everybody else, "I tell you that unless your righteousness surpasses that of the Pharisees and the teachers of the law, you will certainly not enter the kingdom of heaven." Wouldn't it be absurd, in fact, to believe that Jesus came to earth and died on the cross so that we could be *less* faithful to God than the people who lived before Jesus? All in all, tithing in the New Testament turns out to be a *lot more* than we usually want to believe.

So where do all of these competing tensions leave us? Randy Alcorn distills the Bible's teaching about tithing into one simple analogy. He says that the Bible's instructions on tithing are a lot like our state laws on seat belts. If the state suddenly unbuckled the law, would we all immediately unbuckle our belts? Of course not. Seat belts are a good idea whether they're the law or not. And the same thing goes for tithing; tithing is a good idea—tithing is a meaningful guideline—whether it's a law or not. Tithing is what God tells us to do in order to break the spiritual power that Money exerts on us. It's the most potent thing we can do to bring not just the tenth but *all* of our money under the lordship of Christ.

Tithing isn't a grim obligation but a liberating privilege. And because of that, tithing isn't something we can do with a calculator; it's something we have to do with our hearts. One time, a married couple showed me their offering envelope because they wanted me to see that they were tithing $78.26—*exactly* ten percent of their income—every single Sunday. But all I could figure out from their incredible precision was that they had missed the whole point of the exercise. God really doesn't care about the difference between nine percent and eleven percent. What He *does* care about is whether we're breaking free from the influence of Money, and He seems to indicate that giving Him ten percent is a good place to start on that. It seems to me that if we try to give 10.00000 percent, we're just revealing that, for us, the influence of Money is still going strong.

Along the same lines, I talked to a woman once who told me that she'd been tithing faithfully every single week since she got her first job. And she went on to tell me how much fun it was to be able to get the things she wanted when she knew that she had already done her duty and that it didn't matter to God how she used the rest of her income. This woman was completely sincere, but again, she had missed the whole point of tithing. Tithing doesn't compartmentalize money into the fraction that belongs to God and the bulk that belongs to us. Tithing is supposed to help us understand that *all* of our money belongs to God.

A third kind of confused tithing that I've run into seems to happen among church leaders who talk about tithing as if it were God's plan for paying the electric bill at the church. But in the words of Charlie Shedd, "Tithing is not God's way of raising money; tithing is God's way of raising children."

Just as setting aside the Lord's Day each week is a symbol that *all* of our time belongs to God, so setting aside God's tithe each week is a living symbol that *all* of our money belongs to him. In fact, if we give God ten percent, I think it's fair to say that God is more interested in what we keep than in what we've given. The question we're really dealing with is not, "How much of my money will I give to God?" but "How much of God's providence can I keep for myself without getting entangled with another god called Money?"

Tithing isn't intended to be easy; it's intended to be effective. And I've seen it work in my own life and in the lives of others. One of the more dramatic examples that I've seen happened a few years ago when our pastor asked if I would try to ease some of the financial problems that were destroying a marriage in our church. When the estranged couple showed me how much they made, it was obvious that they should have had enough money to make ends meet. But their Money had been barking orders at them for so long that they couldn't even come up with a complete list of their overdue debts anymore.

They couldn't even stop themselves from fighting about it when they were sitting across the coffee table from me.

On one of the evenings when I met with this couple, I gave them a three-ring binder, and I offered to show them how to use it as a family budget book—a spending plan to help them live within their means. For the heading on the first ledger in this notebook, I had already printed the word "Tithe." This couple had never given God anything more than what they happened to have in their wallets when they got to church, and when we figured out what a tithe of their combined incomes would be, I could see them wilt. They couldn't pay their bills when they *weren't* tithing; how could they ever hope to pay their bills if they were?

But I poised my pen over the tithing page in that notebook, and I looked up for permission to write what we had estimated would be ten percent of the couple's income. The husband looked at his wife. The wife looked at her husband. Finally, the husband said, "Nothing else we've ever tried has worked," and he nodded for me to go ahead and fill in the first line of their budget book with an unimaginable tithe of their combined incomes. And as soon as this couple went out the door with their new budget book, I got down on my knees, and I prayed, "Lord, don't fail me now. I've told these people what you've said to do, and if this doesn't work, I've probably just destroyed what little was left of their marriage."

Well, it didn't take long at all for that marriage to split in two. But the two parts that it broke into weren't the two people going their separate ways. No, the two parts that this marriage broke into were the two periods before and after that night when the husband and wife together made a commitment to God in tithing. I don't want to make it sound like any of this was easy; for a long time, the husband had to work two jobs, and the whole family had to get used to some real austerity. But there was a dramatic change in this family as soon as that weekly tithe started to break the spell that Money had cast on them for so long. Instead of having money (small "m" now) tell them what to do, they were suddenly in the position of telling money what to do. And two years later, I got to be a witness when this couple renewed their wedding vows, and I got to eat a piece of wedding cake to celebrate that (except for their exculpatory home loan) this family was completely out of debt.

This is the liberation that comes from living within the biblical paradox of giving. We don't have to worry about taking care of God or building His kingdom for Him. As the Bible says, "Since he is Lord of heaven and earth, . . . human hands can't serve his needs —for he has no needs. He himself gives life and breath to everything, and he satisfies every need" (Acts 17:24–25 NLT). And yet, the God who made the world does long to receive our gifts through His designated receivers. In fact, in Acts 20:35 Paul says, "I showed you that . . . we must help the weak, remembering the words the Lord Jesus himself said: 'It is more blessed to give than to receive.'" Giving is more blessed because giving liberates our hearts in ways that allow God to work in our lives. "'Bring the whole tithe into the storehouse, . . .' says the Lord Almighty, 'and see if I will not throw open the floodgates of heaven'" (Malachi 3:10).

LOOSE CHANGE

The three big questions about tithing

Every time I've spoken in public about tithing, the same three or four questions have always come up. The first one is simple: "Am I supposed to tithe from my gross pay or from my take-home pay?" When people ask this question, it usually shows that they're trying to figure out what's the minimum they can get away with, and if that's their attitude, even tithing from their gross pay isn't going to do them any good. So the best answer I can give to this question is simply another question: "What do you want to surrender to the lordship of Christ—everything you have, or just part of it?

The second perennial question is, "Am I supposed to tithe to my home church, or can I give part of my tithe to other Christ-centered ministries?" There are two schools of thought on this issue. The one that we've already encountered is that we can give to God any time we give to "the least of these," whether we do that through our own churches, through parachurch organizations, or through some other kind of informal giving that doesn't involve any organization at all. That's certainly legitimate, but it can also be awfully unfocused, and studies have shown that people who don't give systematically tend to wildly overestimate how much they've given. On the other hand, there's a very different school of thought that's called the "Storehouse Principle," from the passage in Malachi 3:10 that says, "Bring the whole tithe into the storehouse." If my own local church is the hub of my spiritual growth and activity, then it makes sense for me to think of it as my local branch of God's storehouse and to bring my entire tithe into it. Of course, the Storehouse Principle is a lot more of a doctrine than we can usually get out of one word in the Bible, so I don't think it would be appropriate for us to fight over it. The bottom line is that there are simply two different ways of looking at this question, and the Bible doesn't take a completely firm stand on one way or the other. In my mind, the best way to resolve this little paradox is for each of us to bring the full tithe into the storehouse of our own local churches, and then support other Christ-centered ministries by giving *beyond a tithe*.

The third inevitable question about tithing is a lot like the second one: "Am I supposed to put my entire tithe into the general budget of the church, or can I designate part of my tithe for the ministries (music, Sunday school, missions) that are closest to my heart?" If there's any biblical answer to this question, it would be in a fleeting passage from Acts 4:34–35 that says, "From time to time, those who owned lands or houses sold them, brought the money from the sales, and *put it at the apostles' feet*, and it was distributed to anyone as he had need." In other words, the members of the early church didn't designate where their gifts should go; they trusted the church leaders to make those decisions.

Now, assuming that we still have godly leaders in our churches today, it seems wise that the leaders—who have the most spiritual maturity, and who have the most relevant training, and who know the most about the prevailing needs—should be the ones to make the most difficult decisions about how a congregation divides its resources. And as a side note, it seems really inappropriate for us to engrave bronze plaques with the names of people who've designated their money for special projects while nobody gets singled out for the ministry of roof repairs or the sacrifice of paper towels in the bathrooms.

When people are sincerely trying to reform after years of poor stewardship, there's a fourth question about tithing that sometimes comes up: "Should I start to tithe when I'm still delinquent on my debts?" It's certainly not a good witness to our long-suffering creditors if we say, "I can't pay what I owe because I'm paying my tithe to God." On the other hand, if the liberation of tithing isn't for the people who've fallen head-over-heels into debt, I don't know who it *is* for. Sometimes there's just no good way to get out of a bad situation, and if we simply don't have the means to tithe and to stay current on our payments at the same time, it may be that the best we can do is to take a sincere first step in the right direction on both accounts. Be honest with God. Be honest with creditors. Persevere until both have received what they are due. As the Bible says in Galatians 6:9, "Let us not become weary in doing good, for at the proper time we will reap a harvest, if we do not give up."

Tithing as a weapon

Let's admit it: Sometimes when people designate their offerings for their own pet projects, or when they divert their offerings to ministries outside of their own churches, what they are really trying to do is block the plans and the priorities of their church leaders. We've all heard these kinds of tactics a hundred times: "I don't think we really need to convert the courtyard into an atrium, so I'm going to designate all of my giving for foreign missions." The first problem with this time-honored technique is that it doesn't work. I don't know of any church where there's somebody assigned to monitor every member's giving and figure out what policies each member likes or doesn't like. But the more troubling thing about manipulative giving is that it isn't Christlike. Sometimes it might be necessary to "speak the truth in love" to misguided church leaders; Jesus himself certainly "spoke the truth in love" when He overturned the tables of the moneychangers. But Jesus didn't let that kind of concern get tangled up with our giving to God. Near the end of Mark 12, Jesus really lambasts some church leaders for devouring "the widows' houses" (v. 40). He says that the leaders had been accepting sacrificial gifts from old ladies and spending the money on their own long robes and banquets. Now, it can't be a coincidence that the very next paragraph of the gospel is the story of the old widow bringing her last two coins to a collection box that was administered by the very church leaders Jesus had just been criticizing. If I had been there, I probably would have tried to stop the old girl. I would have told her to divert her giving to the Zacchaeus Endowment for the Poor or the Good Samaritan's Foundation for Victims of Crime. But in the gospel story, Jesus doesn't try to stop the old widow from dropping her last two coins into the general fund. Quite the opposite, he commends her—lavishly, in fact. Jesus loves the cheerful giver—not the gift that's wielded as a weapon.

"Bring the firstfruits of our dough" (Nehemiah 10:37, KJV)

In the Bible, the word *tithe* describes "the *quantity* of our gifts to God," and the word *firstfruits* describes "their *quality.*" We don't bring God the leftovers; we bring Him the first and the best of everything we have.

In Old Testament times, the idea of bringing the firstfruits to God was a lot more radical than we can really appreciate. In a country where most people lived by farming, God's people gave Him the firstfruits of their crops before they knew for sure if they were going to have any "secondfruits." About the closest we can come to that today is to give the first tenth of our paychecks to God and not wait to see what may or may not be left over at the end of the month.

But the step that's really beyond bringing God the *first* of everything is to bring him the *best* of everything. When my wife and I got married, her old widowed Aunt Catherine wanted to give us a very special wedding present, so she invited us to come to her house and pick out one of the paintings that her late husband, the very talented Uncle Douglas, had created as a hobby. We knew that in Aunt Catherine's closets there were boxes full of wonderful paintings, but Aunt Catherine insisted that we should walk around her house and take one of the framed pictures off the wall. She explained, "If it wasn't a picture that I wanted to keep, it wouldn't be good enough for me to give." That's the real essence of firstfruits. It's not enough for us to give God the first of everything we have; we need to give Him the very things we most want to keep for ourselves.

Hiring the Good Samaritan

It's interesting that in English the two commodities that we can "spend" are time and money—and the odd difference between them is that the richest person in the world doesn't have any more time to spend than the poorest. We honor God by "spending time" in Christ-centered ministries, just the way we honor God by "spending money" on those same endeavors. But there's a problem when we try to use one kind of spending as a substitute for the other. We know it's futile for a Disneyland Daddy to spend money on his kids as a substitute for spending time with them, but there are people who think it makes sense to spend money on paying the Good Samaritan so that they don't have to spend time in the work of ministry. On the flip side, there are probably more people who think they can spend time in church work as a substitute for giving. We have the expression, "Time is money," but the two commodities aren't really interchangeable. The Bible doesn't instruct us to give God our time *or* money—but our time *and* money.

Generous to a fault

One Saturday quite a few years ago, I was driving down a street called Mitchell Avenue when a disheveled woman stepped into the street in front of me. She was waving her arms and pleading for help. She told me that she had just been evicted from her apartment, and she had put what little money she had left into gasoline so she could drive to her sister's house. But now her car had broken down, she was stranded, and she didn't know where she would end up spending the night. I asked her if I could give her enough money for a Greyhound ticket so she could at least get to her sister's house that night. The woman looked up to heaven, and she started to cry, and she said, "Thank you, Jesus; I prayed that you would help me, and you did."

A few years later, a friend of mine told me that he'd been driving down Mitchell Avenue when a disheveled woman stepped into the street in front of him, waving her arms and pleading for help. She'd been evicted, broken down, and stranded, and she'd been moved to tears by her gratitude to Jesus when my friend helped her with bus fare.

Some people might conclude from a story like this that we should never give money to a panhandler. But God gave us the gift of his Son, knowing in advance that we were going to abuse the gift. So, if we're also abused occasionally when we give in the name of Jesus, we'll be in extraordinarily good company. Naturally, we ought to be careful not to let ourselves be hoodwinked out of what God has entrusted to us. But when there's doubt, it seems most Christlike to err occasionally on the side of generosity. Spiritually, it's much less dangerous to risk being cheated than to risk being hardened to the sufferings of others. And even if we discover later that we've been conned, we won't have anything to regret. When God ultimately separates the sheep from the goats, He may just smile and say to us, "Well done, good and faithful servants; you were generous to a fault."

The OBOBFAMBOW

Some years ago, I was part of a church that tried to put together enough money on a single Sunday morning to build a house for doctors at a mission clinic in

Honduras. On the Sunday of the "Offering Beyond Our Budget for a Mission Beyond Our Walls," there happened to be a medical student spending her spring break in Honduras helping out at the clinic. This woman was a very admirable humanitarian but a very bitter critic of everything Christian. As it turned out, on the morning of the OBOBFAMBOW, our congregation "accidentally" overshot the goal, and we gathered enough money not only to build the house but also to provide appliances for it. I found out later that when our news reached the clinic by satellite phone, our humanitarian critic was flabbergasted. She wasn't driven to her knees to accept Christ, but she was driven to press her nose against the windows of the kingdom to try to figure out what's been happening to us inside.

The apostle Paul wrote, "Because of the service by which you have proved yourselves, men will praise God for the obedience that accompanies your confession of the gospel of Christ, and for your generosity in sharing with them and with everyone else" (2 Corinthians 9:13). That medical student in Honduras wasn't interested in hearing anybody's "confession of the gospel of Christ," but because of the "service by which we proved ourselves," she was awed by "the *obedience* that accompanied our confession." The Bible explains it this way: "This service that you perform is not only supplying the needs of God's people but is also overflowing in many expressions of thanks to God" (2 Corinthians 9:12). When this special offering brought glory to God, it wasn't just a good thing that we decided to do; it was *the* good thing that we were created to do. Paul says, in fact, that "We who first hoped in Christ have been destined and appointed to live for the praise of his glory" (Ephesians 1:12 RSV).

NEGOTIABLES

Paying the tithe

We've seen that Malachi 3 says, "Bring the full tithe into the storehouse." The action word in that sentence is obviously *bring*. In other tithing passages from assorted translations of the Bible, tithes are *set aside, presented, offered, gathered, collected,* and even *paid*. The only mention of a tithe ever being *given* is in Luke 18:11–12 where a first-class hypocrite prays, "God, I thank you that I'm not like other men . . . I *give* a tenth of all I get." What does the Bible's choice of verbs tell us about God's attitude toward the tithe? Read Malachi 3:6–12, and reflect on these verbs again in light of that passage's withering question, "Will anyone rob God?"

A tithe of the tithe

The Old Testament prescribes that one of the three tithes should go to the Levites, who were essentially the church establishment. Later, in Numbers 18:26, God says to those Levites, "When you receive from the Israelites the tithe that I give you as your inheritance, you must present a tenth of that tithe as the Lord's offering." How might a church today present a tithe of the tithe to the Lord? What might be the consequences of a church doing that?

Six

SPENDING

MATTHEW 21:22 ~ MARK 10:21

If we were moving into the neighborhood of the Three Pigs, would God want us to live in a House of Straw, a House of Sticks, or a House of Bricks?

We don't have to worry about the Big Bad Wolf; Jesus has already taken care of that menace. But when we choose a house in this neighborhood, we still have a big decision to make about how God wants us to live. Does God want us to try to earn so much and then spend so much that we can live in a magnificent House of Bricks? Does he expect us to be content with some dilapidated old House of Straw? Or does God want us to split the difference and settle down somewhere in a nice little House of Sticks? When we're in a position to make lifestyle choices, how much money should we try to earn, and how much of what we earn should we spend on ourselves?

Before I go any further, I should acknowledge that most of the people in the world don't get to make any lifestyle choices at all. We can all name the reasons. The proverbial wars, pestilence, and famine. Dictatorships, genocide, apartheid. Typhoons, earthquakes, wild fires. Even stupidity—American cartoonist Kin Hubbard once said, "I knew a man who was so poor he had 26 dogs." People in these circumstances just don't have much of a choice about their lifestyles. If they get any house at all, it's a House of Straw. But I'm thinking about those of us who have at least some say in how much money we'll try to earn and how much of that money we'll decide to spend on living in a House of Straw or a House of Sticks or a House of Bricks.

A few years ago, a preacher in our neighborhood sent all the neighbors a free copy of his book about lifestyle choices, and he came down firmly on the side of Bricks. This minister quoted the King James translation of Matthew 21:22, where Jesus promises, "Whatsoever ye shall ask in prayer, believing, ye shall receive." We've already seen in Proverbs 10:22 that, "The blessing of the Lord brings wealth, and he adds no trouble to it." And we've already seen in Ecclesiastes 5:19 that, "It is a good thing to receive wealth from God and the good health to enjoy it" (NLT). So this pastor just took the matter one little step farther, and he told us all to pray for what he called "Kingdom Prosperity." Then he went on to explain that if we "ask in prayer, believing," and we *don't* receive Kingdom Prosperity, it'll only be because we haven't believed enough.

Now, there's no question that the Bible says wealth is a blessing from God, but there's still something about Kingdom Prosperity that makes us uncomfortable. In this pastor's book, he talked about praying for big houses and classy cars, and it seemed as if his brand of Kingdom Prosperity had gotten a lot more wrapped up in prosperity than in the kingdom. C. S. Lewis would tell him he had failed to follow the sunbeam back to the sun. Along the same lines, the "Health and Wealth Gospel" always seems to end up more focused on health and wealth than on the gospel. The "Name It and Claim It" catchphrase doesn't even bother to mention anything other than the "It" that we're supposed to name and claim. And the "Live Like a King's Kid" philosophy falls apart as soon as we realize that *the* King's Kid, Jesus Christ, had a lifestyle that was *anything but* what most Christians mean when they use that phrase. Jesus didn't have a House of Bricks. In fact, in Matthew 8:20 Jesus points out that He didn't have a house at all: "Foxes have dens to live in, and birds have nests, but the Son of Man has no place even to lay his head" (NLT).

On top of that, in Mark 4:1–20 Jesus brings up another problem with Kingdom Prosperity. In His parable of the sower, Jesus uses a bag of seed as a symbol of "the word" (v. 20), and He talks about what happens to that seed when it lands in four different places. When the Word of God was scattered into my life, it didn't get snatched away as soon as it landed, like the seed that fell on a path. And for me, the Word didn't shrivel up and die a few weeks later, like the seed that fell in the rocks. But in my life, the Word hasn't exactly produced a great crop either, like the seed that fell on good soil. So the only option that's left is that the Word in my life must be most like the seed that landed in the thorns—the thorns that "choke the word, making it unfruitful" (Mark 4:19). And exactly what are those thorns? Jesus said they are "the worries of this life, the deceitfulness of wealth and the desires for other things" (Mark 4:19). If the deceitfulness of wealth can choke the Word like thorns choke a seedling, then Kingdom Prosperity has a king-sized problem built right into it. In fact, Randy Alcorn tells a story about a church leader from Romania who said, "In my experience, 95 percent of the believers who face the test of persecution will pass it, while 95 percent who face the test of prosperity will fail."

To get away from all the thorns around the House of Bricks, some people have relocated to the House of Straw. I used to follow some daily devotional booklets that came from a saintly church leader at an inner-city ministry. That leader was haunted by the story of how Jesus looked at a rich young man—"and loved him," according to the Bible—and said to him, "One thing you lack . . . Go, sell everything you have and give to the poor, and you will have treasure in heaven. Then come, follow me" (Mark 10:21). And from that one incident in the Bible, this man taught that it's a sin to have money in the bank, it's a sin to have insurance, and it's a sin to have a retirement plan. After all, didn't Jesus say, "Go, sell *everything* you have and give to the poor"?

Now, most people who've opted for a lifestyle of Christian simplicity haven't been quite as extreme as this particular man, but for centuries, there've been Christians who've decided to live in "Voluntary Poverty for the sake of the gospel." One of them, namely Saint Francis, taught that "detachment from material things is the mysterious key to spiritual freedom." And that outlook certainly lines up with the big question that the Bible asks in James 2:5: "Has not God chosen those who are poor in the eyes of the world to be rich in faith and to inherit the kingdom he promised those who love him?" So there's a solid biblical basis for deciding to live in a House of Straw.

Then again, I could probably be the poster child for Voluntary Poverty Anonymous. Forty years ago, when I was in school and thinking about a career, this virtue of Voluntary Poverty for the sake of the gospel was what shaped my thinking. I loved geometry and physics, plus I loved mechanical drawing, so I thought I'd like to be an architect. But at the time, I thought it would be ungodly for me to have the income or the lifestyle that a successful architect might have, and I thought that God would love me more if I would set aside my own ambitions in order to live and work among the poor as an inner-city math teacher.

There was one big wrinkle in that blueprint, though: I absolutely *hated* being an inner-city math teacher. I wasn't temperamentally suited for the job. God had never gifted me to be the Mother Teresa of mathematics, and when I got locked into a room with all those feral teenagers for five periods every day, I wasn't just unhappy; I was suicidal. After five years, I had to give up on my teaching career, but it was quite a few more years after that before I really understood where I'd gone wrong. I finally realized that—just the way Kingdom Prosperity can get more focused on prosperity than on the kingdom—my Voluntary Poverty for the sake of the gospel had gotten more focused on poverty than on the gospel. I thought that poverty itself was the way "to be rich in faith and to inherit the kingdom that God has promised." But if that were the case, Haiti would be the holiest nation in the Western Hemisphere, and all of our slums would be cloisters of righteousness.

Looking back now, I can see that the Bible has always made a distinction between self-denial and self-delusion. In the familiar "Love Chapter," the apostle Paul says, "If I give all I possess to the poor and surrender my body to the flames, but have not love, I gain nothing" (1 Corinthians 13:3). And in Matthew 9:13, Jesus himself says, "Go and learn what this means: 'I desire mercy, not sacrifice.'" In one of his books, M. Scott Peck probes for the real motives behind my kind of self-sacrifice when he asks, "Could it be that the most important thing in your life is to have a sense of moral superiority, and that in order to maintain this sense, you need to be mistreated?" Yikes! That about does it for the House of Straw.

At this point, we're snarled in another biblical paradox. We've seen that there are Bible passages that favor the House of Bricks, and there are other passages that favor the House of Straw. But there are also all kinds of passages that pretty well bulldoze both of those houses. So if the Three Pigs can get any guidance from the Three Bears, maybe it's time for us to give up on the House of Bricks that was too rich, and the House of Straw that was too poor, and to settle down in the House of Sticks where everything will be just right.

Here again, there's a really solid biblical basis for this choice. In Proverbs 30:8–9, the writer says to God, "Give me neither poverty nor riches, but give me only my daily bread. Otherwise, I may have too much and disown you and say, 'Who is the Lord?' Or I may become poor and steal, and so dishonor the name of my God." We probably haven't consciously picked that verse as the motto of our lifestyle choices, but for most of us, that's exactly what we've fallen into by default. We've chosen to live in the nice-enough-but-not-too-lavish House of Sticks.

But wait just a minute here, because setting our sights on the House of Sticks leaves us with two other gigantic problems. The first one is that, again and again, God has worked out His purposes by making some people fantastically rich. In the Old Testament, that was certainly the case for leaders like Abraham and Joseph and Solomon. And in the New Testament, when he signs off from his letter to the Ephesians, Paul writes, "Aquila and [his wife] Priscilla greet you warmly in the Lord, and so does the church *that meets at their house*" (1 Corinthians 16:19). If the whole congregation at Ephesus could fit into Priscilla and Aquila's living room, we'd have to assume that they lived in a House of Bricks. And if we never aspire to anything more than an ordinary House of Sticks, how do we know that we're not cutting ourselves off from what God may have wanted to accomplish by giving us Kingdom Prosperity?

On the flip side, the other problem with setting our sights on the House of Sticks is that God also determines that some people will be dirt poor. It's really hard to be a successful prophet if you have to run home for supper every night after work, but you can lambast kings as much as God tells you to when the only supper you're going to get anyway is a few locusts with wild honey. The word *apostle* means "one who is sent," and part of what changed Jesus' disciples into His apostles was what they said to Him in Luke 18:28, "We have left all we had to follow you." And as for Jesus himself, once He left His carpentry shop, He was as poor as a synagogue mouse. Everything He owned in the world was divvied up in a quick dice game at the foot of the cross. If we're never willing to give up a comfortable House of Sticks, then there'll be a limit to how much we can be like Jesus.

So moving into a middling House of Sticks doesn't resolve the biblical paradox between Kingdom Prosperity and Voluntary Poverty for the sake of the gospel. "Moderation in all things" might be a good motto for weight control, but when we try to split the difference between poverty and prosperity, all we end up with is mediocrity. And even though Revelation 3:16 doesn't really talk about lifestyle choices, it does tell us that mediocrity makes Jesus sick. Several of the lesser-known translations of the Bible actually render Jesus' words as, "Because you are lukewarm and neither hot nor cold, before long I will *vomit* you out of my mouth."

What we really have here, then, is a triple-whammy paradox, and it's about enough to make us evacuate the whole neighborhood. At one end of the block, Kingdom Prosperity could be doing great things with God, but it's partying in the House of Bricks. On the other side of the tracks, Voluntary Poverty could also be doing great things with God, but it's too busy flagellating itself in the House of Straw. And right in the middle of the road, in the House of Sticks, we're not really accomplishing much of anything with Jesus, and it looks like He's reaching for the Pepto-Bismol. This isn't the biggest triune paradox in the Bible, but it's a doozy. And how are we ever going to embrace all three faces of this paradox at the same time?

The real root of this predicament is that the Bible has so much to say about money. Randy Alcorn has counted that there are 2,350 Bible verses about money—and he's discovered that this is about twice as many verses as there are about faith and prayer combined. Almost all of Jesus' parables deal with money or possessions in one way or another. The parables talk about salt, grain, yeast, vineyards, pearls, loaves, wineskins, nets, oil lamps, fig trees, mustard seeds, hidden treasures, lost coins, extra barns, great banquets, lost sheep, and invested "talents." They deal with servants, tenants, homeowners, thieves, moneylenders, shrewd managers, wasteful sons, rich men and beggars, wise and foolish builders, and employers with some really unorthodox ideas about managing a payroll. If only there were *something* that Jesus had talked about more than money, that something might be the key to resolving our three-way paradox of Straw, Sticks, and Bricks.

I'd be embarrassed to admit how long it took me to realize just how obvious the *something* is that outshines everything Jesus had to say about money. For years, I had quoted other people's statistics about how often Jesus mentions money in the parables. But then one night, I sat down and actually read what Jesus *said* in His parables, all of them at once, and this is what I found: "The kingdom of heaven is like a man who sowed good seed" (Matthew 13:24). "The kingdom of heaven is like a mustard seed" (v. 31). "The kingdom of heaven is like yeast" (v. 33). "The kingdom of heaven is like treasure hidden in a field" (v. 44). "The kingdom of heaven is like a merchant looking for fine pearls" (v. 45). "The kingdom of heaven is like

a king who wanted to settle accounts with his servants"
(18:23). "The kingdom of heaven is like a net let down
into the lake" (13:47). "The kingdom of heaven is like a
king who prepared a wedding banquet for his son" (22:2).
"The kingdom of heaven will be like ten virgins who took
their lamps and went out to meet the bridegroom" (25:1).
The kingdom of heaven is "like a man going on a jour-
ney" (25:14).

Jesus' parables aren't centered on money and possessions at all. Jesus does talk *a lot* about money and possessions in His parables, but that's only because, as someone
has said, "money is the barometer of the soul." Talking
about money and possessions helps us measure where
our souls are. But what's really important to Jesus is not
money and possessions, but the kingdom, the kingdom,
and the kingdom. Jesus' ambition for us isn't a House of
Straw, a House of Sticks, *or* a House of Bricks. It's the
kingdom of heaven—a house not built with hands.

I'm not the only one who's ever gotten excited by real-
izing how central the kingdom of God is in our understanding of money and possessions. In the gospel of Luke,
somebody hears Jesus talking about this idea, and he gets
so excited that he blurts out, "Blessed is the man who will
eat at the feast in the kingdom of God" (Luke 14:15). And
that's when Jesus starts telling His story about people who
were invited to just such a feast. "They all alike began to
make excuses," according to Jesus. "The first said, 'I have
just bought a field, and I must go and see it. Please excuse

me.' Another said, 'I have just bought five yoke of oxen, and I'm on my way to try them out. Please excuse me'" (Luke 14:18–19). We could imagine another person who said, "I'm busy looking for Kingdom Prosperity. Please excuse me." Or another person may have said, "I'm busy looking for Voluntary Poverty for the sake of the gospel. Please excuse me." There are many things—even seemingly good things like self-sacrifice—that we can want more than we want the kingdom. But in Matthew 6:33, Jesus puts them all in their place: "Seek first [God's] kingdom and his righteousness, and all these things will be given to you as well."

Even the grammar in that monumental verse is instructive. The first half of the sentence is in the active voice: Get busy and "*seek* first [God's] kingdom." But the second half of the sentence is in the passive voice: Just wait, and "all these things *will be given* to you as well." And just what are all these other things that we should expect God to give to us when we seek first His kingdom? Will they be things that give us Kingdom Prosperity? Or circumstances that put us into Voluntary Poverty for the sake of the gospel? Or something in between? We can't really predict. Proverbs 22:2 explains, "Rich and poor have this in common: The Lord is the Maker of them all."

Some people who seek first the kingdom of God are going to end up living in an unremarkable House of Sticks, for the sake of that kingdom. To these people, the Bible says, "Make it your ambition to lead a quiet life, to mind your own business and to work with your hands, just as we told you, so that your daily life may win the respect of outsiders, and so that you will not be dependent on anybody" (1 Thessalonians 4:11–12). When we're called by God to live in a House of Sticks, we aren't being relegated to mediocrity; we're being assigned to a unique mission. We're God's "marketplace missionaries." Our daily labor is in itself an offering to God.

I consider computer programming to be my primary ministry; it's how I use the strongest gifts that God has given me. But beyond our labor itself, God can use His marketplace missionaries at the lunch table at work and over the back fence at home to speak in such a way and to give in such a way and to simply live in such a way that other people will be drawn by God to accept Christ as their Savior and to serve Him as their Lord—people who could never be reached by a pastor or by a televangelist or by a religious tract in the mail.

Other people who seek first the kingdom of God are going to end up living in a meager House of Straw for the sake of that Kingdom. These are the people Jesus was talking to in Luke 6:20 when He said, "Blessed are you who are poor, for yours is the kingdom of God." I have a friend who left what little she had in order to go off and barely subsist as a school teacher on the West Bank in Israel—just so she could be a Christian witness in that troubled corner of the world. One time when she was visiting us, I asked her, "How can you live like that?"

but she just gestured around our living room, and she asked, "How can you live like *this*?" She said, "I have everything I want, and I'm just doing what I want to do." The Bible would say that she was "poor, yet making many rich; having nothing, and yet possessing everything" (2 Corinthians 6:10).

Still other people who seek first the kingdom of God are going to end up living in a luxurious House of Bricks for the sake of that kingdom. "For everything God created is good," Paul writes, "and nothing is to be rejected if it is received with thanksgiving" (1 Timothy 4:4). I happen to know a modern-day Priscilla and Aquila who were seeking first the kingdom when God decided to bless them with real Kingdom Prosperity. Their children were teenagers at the time, and this couple used their prosperity to turn their home into a place where all the kids in the neighborhood wanted to hang out. They had a tennis court and an inground swimming pool in their backyard, and they even had a little dumbwaiter in the wall from the kitchen to the family room, just to bring food down and to take dirty dishes back up. That family room became the meeting place for the Young Life ministry in their school district, and after all the beach towels had been tossed into the dryer, and all the dirty dishes had been cranked back up to the kitchen, dozens of young people (who may have never encountered Christ in any other place) had encountered Him there in that appealing House of Bricks. The apostle Paul must have been speaking like a Young Life leader to people like these kingdom-seeking friends of mine when he wrote, "You will be made rich in every way so that you can be generous on every occasion, and through us your generosity will result in thanksgiving to God" (2 Corinthians 9:11).

At this point, we've revisited the House of Straw, the House of Sticks, and the House of Bricks, and we've seen that every one of them can be a sanctified place to live if we're seeking first the kingdom of God. But there's still one more option that doesn't occur to most of us, and to understand that fourth lifestyle choice, we need to think for a minute about the people who are exceptionally rich.

When we try to name the richest people in the world, we all think of movie stars and business tycoons, oil sheiks and the Queen of England. But when I saw a graph of the economic spectrum of the whole planet, I realized that those billionaires are so few and so rich that they're not even on the chart. They're somewhere way off the edge of the paper. So in order to come up with a realistic list of who's rich in this world, we'll have to look among the wealthiest people who are still on the chart. I could cite statistics about this all day, but there's one very simple statistic that tells me everything I really need to know: I've read that three-quarters of the families on earth will never own a car in any condition. But in the thirty-odd years of our marriage, my wife and I have owned *twelve* cars. We're "just" a computer programmer and an English teacher, and we think of our salaries and our subcompact cars as pretty modest by American standards. But by any global standard, my wife and I are some of the richest people in human history.

We know that wealth is a gift from God, but for those of us who've had the means to drive more than one car, the "deceitfulness of wealth, and the desires for other things" (Mark 4:19) aren't just a couple of carpet tacks that might have been dropped in the straight and narrow road that leads to life; they're a couple of Stop Sticks that have been tossed right under our tires. And before we career off the pavement, we'd better stop and ask ourselves what God is really trying to accomplish by making us the stewards of so much. In Luke 12:48, Jesus says, "When someone has been given much, much will be required in return" (NLT). So we need to consider the possibility that what God wants from us rich people is something "much more" than yet another sanctified House of Bricks.

Sometimes, when we see TV images of war refugees and child prostitutes, sweatshop workers and deranged vagrants, tsunami victims and AIDS orphans, we wonder why God hasn't provided for them the way He's provided for us. But the fact of the matter may be that God *has* provided for them; He's provided for *them* by giving money to *us*. God has entrusted us with enough financial power to work miracles—although as renowned educator Jonathan Kozol would say, "We pretend we don't have power so that no one will expect us to use it." But if we're

honest before God, we'll have to recognize that the fourth
option in the neighborhood of Straw, Sticks, and Bricks
is this: Some of us who seek first the kingdom of God are
going to end up with enough money to live in a House
of Bricks, but God is going to ask us to live somewhere
more modest and to share lavishly from the resulting sur-
pluses—not because we feel guilty but because we feel
"blessed to be a blessing."

Stewardship expert Richard Towner calls this "driving your stake"—pegging your lifestyle in place so that
as your income increases your giving can increase also
but your lifestyle can't start slithering along with it. A lot
more people are probably called to this option than want
to recognize it. There's absolutely nothing wrong with
spending money on a House of Bricks for the sake of the
kingdom—but that's not the only way God can use our
Kingdom Prosperity.

Regardless of whether we're trying to live beneath our
means or just trying to live *within* our means, we need the
contentment to pray, "Give us this day our daily bread."
But those words "daily bread" open up another whole set
of questions, don't they? Some people have paraphrased
the Lord's Prayer to say, "Give us this day the things we
need." But how can we distinguish what we really need
from what we only want—and what we legitimately want
from what we selfishly desire? When Henry David Thoreau lived at Walden Pond, he wrote that the only things
we really need are food, clothing, shelter, and (in the

Massachusetts winter) some kind of fuel. But a few years after he wrote those words, Thoreau died of tuberculosis. Maybe he needed health care too.

A century later, psychologist Abraham Maslow came up with a little better understanding of our needs. Maslow noticed that things such as food, clothing, and shelter are just our most basic needs, and once those needs have been satisfied, other needs emerge. One really basic example of Maslow's theory is that, if people are starving, they'll do dangerous things to get food, but once they've been fed, the same people will feel a real need for safety. Once people are safe, they'll feel a need for companionship. Once they have companionship, they'll feel all kinds of other needs. Now, I know that Abraham Maslow never claimed to be a Christian, and I'm not going to try to explain all human motivations as some kind of animal instincts, but I do think that Maslow showed us where Thoreau went wrong. Most of our needs aren't quite as crucial as food, clothing, and shelter, and we usually think of the higher needs as "wants," but God knows that our lives would be incomplete without them. We really need music and things of beauty, for example, even though we could survive without them. We need variety. We need mental stimulation. I don't think it's too much of a stretch to say that at least some people need to have pets. We even need to have fun, and the only problem with that need is that sometimes we don't know whether "fun" means a yoyo or a yacht.

When we're trying to make decisions about what we should acquire, it's important to understand that we can't distinguish a need from a want or a desire by looking at a price tag, or even by studying the object we're longing for. Here's one example: To a person who's on the waiting list to get a kidney transplant, a cell phone to carry around is a basic necessity of life. To my wife, driving alone for three hundred miles to visit her mother on a dark winter night, a cell phone is a perfectly reasonable thing to want. But to me, driving back and forth to work every day on a route that I could walk if I had to, a cell phone would be a ridiculous desire. The distinction between a need, a want, and a desire isn't based on the object that we're longing for, but on the impulse behind our longing. It's the motive—not the merchandise.

I talked to a man once who couldn't get his car into his two-car garage because there was hardly enough room in there to walk between his two table saws, his band saw, his jig saw, his drill press, his planer, his lathe, and his workbench piled with hand tools. I can't read minds, so I really wasn't trying to judge whether all of these tools were needs or wants or foolish desires. But for some reason, this man felt compelled to tell me that every year he builds a rocking chair to sell in his church's bazaar—as if that somehow justified his garage full of machinery. What he didn't understand is that when we spend money with the right motives, when we spend money on our God-given needs and wants, and when we spend money in harmony with God's kingdom principles, then we don't need to toss in any kind of a churchy consideration to justify our purchases.

The apostle Paul writes, "Whoever does not provide for relatives, and especially for family members, has denied the faith and is worse than an unbeliever" (1 Timothy 5:8 NRSV). When we spend money on the needs and the godly wants of our families, then we're simply being obedient to this verse of the Bible, and that makes our spending every bit as holy as our giving. And for that matter, when we earn money in ways that are obedient to God's Word, then our *earning* is every bit as holy as our giving.

When we're evaluating a purchase or any kind of a lifestyle expense, the question we need to ask ourselves is not, "Can I figure out any way to justify this purchase by using it in some kind of ministry?" No, the decision isn't that simple. John Wesley preached that three of the questions we should really ask ourselves are these: (1) Am I acting, not as an owner, but as a steward of my Lord's goods? (2) Am I incurring this expense in obedience to God's Word? (3) Do I have reason to believe that, for this very expense, I will be rewarded at the resurrection of the righteous?

A few years ago, when my wife had a birthday while she was going through chemotherapy, I knew I needed help keeping the day cheerful. So I invited a few of our friends who had lived through cancer to come to our house, and I went out and bought my wife what may have been the most extravagant Opera Cream birthday cake in human history. "Do I have reason to believe that, for this very expense, I will be rewarded at the resurrection of the righteous?" Yes. I do.

On the other hand, one evening, when I was standing in the checkout line of a hardware store, I was clutching a rake that wasn't all beat up like the two rakes I already own. And the store should have had more cash registers open, because in the few minutes that I had to wait in line, I had a chance to ask myself that same question, "Do I have reason to believe that, for this very expense, I will be rewarded at the resurrection of the righteous?" And I turned around and put my desire back on the rack. The problem with my shopping trip wasn't that I wanted too much; it was that I almost settled for too little. I almost used some of God's money in a way that would have only increased my attachment to things that can't last. But when I saw my purchase from an eternal perspective, I was content with what I already have in my little House of Sticks; and the Bible says that "Godliness with contentment is great gain" (1 Timothy 6:6).

Different people are assigned to different outcomes. The House of Straw, the House of Sticks, and the House of Bricks can all be God-honoring habitats for people who seek first the kingdom of God and His righteousness. In Ecclesiastes 7:14, Solomon says, "In the day of prosperity be happy, but in the day of adversity consider—God has made the one as well as the other" (NASB). And in Philippians 4:12–13, Paul writes, "I know what it is to be in need, and I know what it is to have plenty. I have learned the secret of being content in any and every situation, whether well fed or hungry, whether living in plenty or in want. I can do everything through him who gives me strength."

LOOSE CHANGE

What about that rich young man?

We brought up the rich young man in Mark 10:17–31, but we left him hanging after Jesus told him to, "Go, sell *everything* you have and give to the poor." Among all of the "hard sayings of Jesus," this is one of the hardest. But before we jump to too many conclusions, let's take another look at how Jesus happened to make this demand.

The rich young man was the one who started this conversation by asking Jesus, "What must I do to inherit eternal life?" (v. 17). Jesus told him that he had to obey the commandments, which gave the rich young man a perfect chance to admit that he was a sinner who needed a Savior. But instead, the rich young man boasted that he had kept all the commandments "since I was a boy" (v. 20). If I can take the liberty of paraphrasing what Jesus said next, it was essentially, "That's great—then the rest of this will be easy: Go sell everything you have, and give to the poor." The look on the young man's face exposed the fact that he hadn't even obeyed the *first* commandment, "You shall have no other gods before me." To this rich young man, the god of Money was still more important than the God of mercy. And the Bible says that the rich young man "went away sorrowful, for he had great possessions" (v. 22 NKJV).

I don't think Jesus' statement to the rich young man is a universal mandate for the rest of us to sell everything we have. Jesus didn't expect that from most of his closest followers. At the same time, Jesus' challenge to the rich young man *is* a universal mandate to put God ahead of everything that this world has to offer.

As for the rich young man himself, all we know is that by the end of the story he had turned into the *sorrowful* rich young man. We're left to suppose that he eventually went on to become the sorrowful rich *old* man—and ultimately, the sorrowful rich *dead* man.

Solving the problem of Too Much

The American solution to the problem of Too Much is to buy even more. When we're overweight because of too much food, we buy more diet products. And when we run out of closet space because of too much stuff, we rent a bay in a storage facility. God's solution to the problem of Too Much is to give it away. The Bible explains the strategy this way: "Our desire is not that others might be relieved while you are hard pressed, but that there might be equality. At the present time, your plenty will supply what they need, so that in turn their plenty will supply what you need. Then there will be equality, as it is written: 'He who gathered much did not have too much, and he who gathered little did not have too little'" (2 Corinthians 8:13–15).

Graduate from tithing

Those of us who enjoy American prosperity need to decide whether tithing will really be enough to dethrone the industrial-strength god of our extraordinary amounts of Money. After all, tithing is the level of giving that the Bible prescribes for the poor, and tithing from a lavish income isn't at all the same kind of sacrifice as tithing from a meager income. If giving away ten percent doesn't seem to be enough to tame the rest of our money, then Ronald Sider suggests an alternative that he calls "graduated tithing." He says that we upscale Americans should identify a base income that would provide for our real needs, and we should tithe from that. Then, if our income is above that base, or if it later grows above that base, we'll be able to get a few more of our godly wants—while at the same time, it won't be any sacrifice at all for us to give away fifteen percent of the next thousand dollars. And twenty percent of the next thousand. And twenty-five percent of the next thousand, until we're ultimately giving away a hundred percent of any further increases we get.

Dr. Sider's arithmetic might be a little bit mechanical, and over the years, we would certainly need to account

for inflation, but the whole point of giving beyond a
tithe is that, instead of letting our Money drag us into an
ever-expanding lifestyle, we can make a Christ-centered
decision to simply say, "Enough is enough." As Randy
Alcorn teaches, "God's extra provision is usually not
intended to raise our standard of living, but to raise our
standard of giving." When I've spoken to other people
who've experimented with giving beyond a tithe, every
one of them has reported the outcome that Proverbs
11:24 would have predicted: "Some give freely, yet grow
all the richer; others withhold what is due, and only suffer want" (NRSV).

Tithes, offerings, and sacrifices

It seems to me that our needs, wants, and desires
may have parallels in our tithes, offerings, and sacrifices.
When we squelch our selfish desires, we find that it's
really no problem for us to tithe. When we set aside some
of our godly wants, we can give offerings beyond a tithe.
And when we give up some of our own basic needs, we
can give sacrifices that go even beyond tithes and offerings. By these definitions, I know that I've never given a
sacrifice—but the practice of sacrifice is as familiar to us
as our mothers' arms.

The desires of our hearts

In a dictionary of New Testament terms, I can see
that what chokes out the Word in Mark 4:19 is our

passionate desire (*epithumia*) for other things. In Matthew 5:28, it's the same thing that causes men to commit adultery in their hearts: looking at women with passionate desire (*epithumia*). But in Philippians 1:23, it's also the same thing that makes Paul realize that to die is gain—his passionate desire (*epithumia*) to be with the Lord. And in 1 Peter 1:12, it's the same thing again that angels experience when they hear about the gospel—a passionate desire (*epithumia*) to look into these things.

So our real strangler isn't our passionate desires but our *misdirected* passionate desires. And our goal isn't to be *purged* of passionate desires but to be *filled* with passionate desires for what God passionately desires. When Psalm 37:4 talks about God giving us "the desires of [our] heart," maybe we should take that to mean not that God will give us the things we desire but that He will shape our desires. "This is the new agreement I will make with the people of Israel, says the Lord," in *The Living Bible*'s paraphrase of Hebrews 8:10. "I will write my laws in their minds so that they will know what I want without my even telling them, and I will write my laws in their hearts so that they will *want* to obey them."

A rival religious view of what constitutes blessedness

There are legions of creative people in the world who have made careers out of trying to get us to ignore the delicate balances of a biblical lifestyle. We call these people the advertising industry. Now, I'm certainly not opposed to advertisements that tell us honestly how one product is better than the others. But I've made a little hobby out of collecting ads that claim a lot more than that. I have one advertisement for a cooking school that promises, "Cake decorating puts more love in your life." I found another ad for a home-improvement center that says, "Let's build the good life together." And I have an ad for a lead-crystal punch bowl that claims, "In a room with a thing of beauty, you are never truly alone." What poverty! What poverty to think that love can be squeezed from a tube of frosting or companionship from a punch bowl's leaden heart.

Richard Foster has written, "Advertising is a rival religious view of what constitutes blessedness," and we can see that some advertisements go so far as to actually become *creedal* statements: "We believe in Liz Claiborne," for one example. Somebody cautioned me once that I was pushing this insight a little bit too far when I started intoning, "We believe in Liz Claiborne, the clothier almighty, maker of purses and shoes." But the next Easter Sunday, when I unfolded the morning paper, the first thing that caught my eye was an advertising supplement that screamed its Resurrection Day message: "Viva Liz"—Liz Claiborne is alive.

Richard Foster offers some ideas to help us preserve our steward relationship with God while we're being pummeled with advertising messages: (1) Don't unnecessarily expose yourself to "rival religious views" by mall-walking or window-shopping or Web-surfing or wish-book flipping. (2) Train your family to greet television commercials with sarcasm. (3) Avoid the influence of advertising while you're deciding what you really need, and then consult advertisements only to begin your comparison shopping.

Let the rats win

Covetousness is another great enemy of stewardship, and in our society, there's a tremendous pressure to "keep up with the Joneses." I knew a seventh-grade girl who lived in a ten-room house in suburbia and had all the blessings of good schools, music lessons, pets, orthodontia, sports teams, and more than one computer in her home—and I happened to hear her when she came home from a friend's house whining, "It's not fair; Susan has a walk-in closet, and I don't." I want to be quick to point out that the opposite attitude wouldn't be any better; it's not in any way more Christian to detest wealth and to pride ourselves on how *little* we possess.

What *is* Christian is to stop comparing ourselves with other people and to stop considering other people's evaluation of us. Matthew 11:18 says, "For John [the Baptist] came neither eating nor drinking, and [the people] say, 'He has a demon.' The Son of Man came eating and drinking, and they say, 'Here is a glutton and a drunkard.'" Given the track record of these human evaluations of lifestyle choices, I think it would be safe for us to ignore what other people think and what other people have. Ecclesiastes 4:6 says, "Better one handful with tranquility than two handfuls with toil and chasing after the wind." In the rat race of American life, it might be best to just let the rats win.

Disciples commissioned to go home

God calls some people to be great preachers like Peter. And God calls other people to be great missionaries like Paul. But God has called me to be something more like the Gerasene demoniac. Here's a man whose life was completely transformed by an encounter with Jesus, and at the end of the story, Mark records that he was "*imploring* [Jesus] that he might accompany Him" (Mark 5:18 NASB). But Jesus said to him, "Go home" (v. 19). Of course, Jesus didn't say, "Go home and forget everything that happened." He said, "Go home to your people and report to them what great things the Lord has done for you, and how He had mercy on you" (v. 19).

I went through the four gospels once, just looking for every place where Jesus invites somebody to "Follow me" and every place where Jesus tells somebody else to "Go home." I found that the score is about even. As Randy Alcorn explains, "The majority of Christ's followers did not rid themselves of all their possessions, nor were they expected to do so. There were two callings of Christ— one to leave family and possessions behind and one to go back to them. But both callings served the same ultimate purpose—the glory of God and the advancement of His kingdom."

NEGOTIABLES

A summer house of sticks

Suppose we have some friends who are thinking about buying a log cabin on a lake as a summer retreat for their children and their grandchildren, and they've asked for our advice. What questions could we ask that would help them make a godly decision?

Worldly discontentment or godly ambition

Some Christians who are trying to "seek first the kingdom of God and his righteousness" may think it's necessary for them to set aside any worldly ambitions. While it's certainly true that the kingdom of God should be more important to us than career advancement, it's also true that God wants believers to rise to positions of authority in business, in education, in the media, and maybe even in government. What specific hallmarks would help us distinguish worldly discontentment from godly ambition?

Seven

WELL FIXED

EPHESIANS 2:8-9 ~ MATTHEW 16:27

Let's face it: Some people around us aren't playing by the rules, and they're getting away with it. Some athletes have injected more steroids than God ever intended their bodies to have, and their King Kong muscles have catapulted them into the record books. And in the same way, some of our neighbors have held onto more money than God ever intended them to use. They've spent the money they were supposed to share. They're treating the earth "and the fullness thereof" as if it belonged to them— and they're getting away with it. They're buying the stuff we've denied ourselves. Their kids have the stuff our kids envy. It's aggravating.

If it's any consolation, God does seem to understand our aggravation. In one of the psalms, the writer says, "I envied the arrogant when I saw the prosperity of the wicked . . . Always carefree, they increase in wealth" (Psalm 73:3, 12). We're

just like the writer of that psalm when we get indignant about trying to play by the Book while the cheaters are getting ahead of us in the game. But the psalmist goes on to say, "Surely, [Lord,] you place them on slippery ground" (Psalm 73:18). After all, even anabolic steroids have that nasty little side effect of making athletes drop dead at about the age of forty-six.

So here we sit. We know that Romans 12:2 says, "Do not conform any longer to the pattern of this world, but be transformed by the renewing of your mind." In order to not conform to this world's pattern, we've refused to go along with the ways other people use their money, and we've been dutifully sifting through these mind-bogging paradoxes from the Bible. We've realized that there's really nothing in this "stewardship" arrangement for God, and that the benefits are all ours. But still, sometimes the benefits seem pretty scanty compared to what our neighbors are getting, and we can't help asking, "What's in this for me?" In Jeremiah 29:11, God said to the Israelites, "I know the plans I have for you, . . . plans to prosper you and not to harm you, plans to give you hope and a future." But when are God's plans going to take effect for us, and just how is God planning to "prosper" us?

Our rewards may not be quite as distant as they seem. To begin with, stewardship liberates us, and that happens right away. A German theologian named Eberhard Arnold once wrote that, "The drifting balloon is not free. There is no freedom in being stirred by every opinion, steered by every spirit of the times, governed by every urge of instinct. Freedom is there only where a holy moral imperative and a mature will can show us the way we must steer our lives." And Frank Laubach said essentially the same thing a little more concisely when he wrote, "Glad obedience to duty is the only real liberty."

One spring when the Ohio River was flooded, I happened to be walking close to the riverbank, and about seventy-five feet out in the muddy water, I saw a sign sticking up that said, "No Parking." The liberty that comes from glad obedience to God's financial precepts is like the liberty that comes from glad obedience to that No Parking sign. *Not* obeying wouldn't be liberty; it would be insanity. That No Parking sign and God's financial precepts are backed up by laws of nature. When we obey God's precepts, we're living in harmony with creation instead of trying to live in opposition to it. And the reward for doing that is built right into the act of obedience. When we obey a No Parking sign that's already engulfed in a flood, we can drive home and tell the story. And when we follow the "holy moral imperative" to save some of our money, we can coast right through the burned out hot water heaters of life without even being flustered. When we borrow only according to God's principles, we can laugh off the bookkeeping mix-up that triggers the only call we'll ever get from a collection agency. When we give openhandedly, we can break free from the tyranny that Money tries to exert over us. A scientific study by somebody named Stephen Post actually found that, "People who contribute regularly to charities enjoy better health." When we let God direct our lifestyles, we can be as carefree as the young couple who told me that, after their first few years of marriage, they decided that the wife would quit her job and become a full-time mommy. And the next month, their lifestyle without her paycheck wasn't any different from what it had been with her paycheck. Their lifestyle had never been dictated by their double incomes; it had been guided by God. There's freedom, there's security, there's contentment, and there's peace of mind built right into our glad obedience to duty.

But there's more.

We've thought before about Abraham Maslow and how he noticed that when our most basic needs have been satisfied, our higher needs come to the surface. Maslow was a humanist, and for most of his career, he taught that our highest craving is for what he called "self-actualization," or basically just fulfilling our own potential. But when Maslow was getting on in years, he realized that there was still one more undocumented need that was welling up in him. It was a need for what he called "transcendence"—"the need to connect to something beyond the ego."

I know that Maslow would have never described our need for transcendence this way, but I'll say that we all have a thirst to be part of something bigger than ourselves, something more long-lasting than ourselves, something more significant than what the Bible calls our daily routine of "chasing after the wind" (Ecclesiastes 1:14). Some well-intentioned people try to satisfy this thirst for transcendence by pledging to public radio. We Christians satisfy it by pledging to the kingdom of God.

I think about the three women named Mary, Joanna, and Susanna, who seemed to always tag along with Jesus and His disciples. These three probably weren't any more gifted for preaching than I was for high school teaching, but Luke 8:3 says that these women were "contributing their own resources to support Jesus and his disciples" (NLT). Talk about transcendence! These women were bankrolling the redemption of the world.

That opportunity hasn't been closed down. We can still support evangelism and missions, as well as ministries of compassion and healing and justice. On top of that, we can be a direct "means of grace"—a delivery system for God's favor—by the way we share His providence with the people all around us. And isn't it ironic that we usually satisfy our most basic needs by spending on ourselves, but we can satisfy our most elevated needs only by giving to others? This is one of the rewards of stewardship: our thirst for transcendence is satisfied. By "stewarding" everything that God has entrusted to us, we can be part of a movement that has cosmic significance and eternal consequences. Now obviously, money isn't the only tool we can use to "seek first the kingdom of God and his righteousness," but it's one of the most versatile. And in

Matthew 5:6, Jesus says, "Blessed are those who hunger and thirst for righteousness, for they will be filled."

But there's more.

Sometimes, when we obey the financial precepts of God, He comes back to us with some real surprises. In Luke 6:38, Jesus promises, "Give, and it will be given to you. A good measure, pressed down, shaken together and running over, will be poured into your lap." I wonder if this isn't an illustration that Jesus targeted toward the ladies who heard Him preach. I picture a woman getting repaid for a bowl of grain that she gave to a neighbor. The neighbor is refilling the measuring bowl with grain. She presses the grain down and pours in some more. Then she shakes it together and pours in even more. Then the neighbor keeps pouring more grain into the measuring bowl until the woman has to pick up the corners of her apron to catch everything that's getting spilled. "Give, and it will be given to you," Jesus says, "pressed down, shaken together running over into your lap."

God actually dares us to experiment with this promise. The big tithing passage in Malachi has to be the only place in the Bible where it seems as if we're being told, "I double-dog dare you to try this." "'Bring the whole tithe into the storehouse, that there may be food in my house. *Test me in this*,' says the Lord Almighty, 'and see if I will not throw open the floodgates of heaven and pour out so much blessing that you will not have room enough for it'" (Malachi 3:10).

This is another one of those places in Scripture where thinking through what the Bible *doesn't* say helps me understand what the Bible *does* say. So in this passage, I notice that God doesn't say, "I will twist open the faucets of heaven." And He doesn't say, "I will crank open the hydrants of heaven." No, He says, "I will *throw* open the *floodgates* of heaven." He's gonna bust Hoover Dam. He's going to let go of so much blessing that it'll be a danger to everybody downstream. God can't take a chance on releasing this kind of blessing on people who aren't ready to handle it. "If you have not been trustworthy in handling worldly wealth," Jesus asks in Luke 16:11, "who will trust you with true riches?" And one way we demonstrate to God that we're trustworthy in handling worldly wealth is by getting our tithing past the stage of good intentions. So God puts that condition on His promise: *"Bring the whole tithe into the storehouse,* and see if I will not throw open the floodgates of heaven."

In this Malachi passage, though, we also have to notice that God doesn't say He'll pour out so many *dollars* that we won't have room enough for them. He doesn't promise that if I drop my last ten-dollar bill into the offering plate, I'll inherit a fortune a week later from an uncle I never knew. God may do that kind of thing sometimes; I don't know. But that's not what He's promising here. What God *is* promising is to pour out so many *blessings* that we won't have enough room for them, and blessings can come in lots of colors other than green. God can even bless us by *withholding* something we desire, when He knows that this "something" wouldn't work for our eternal good.

I walked right into an example of overflowing blessings once when I dropped something off for one of the elders of our church. I saw that this man and his wife had just knocked out the back wall of their dining room, and they had added about a fifteen-foot extension with big walls of sunshine. The husband explained to me, "In thirty-five years of marriage, we've always tithed. Maybe it's because of that that we've never had any financial problems, and we've never had an argument about money. And maybe tithing has something to do with why all of our kids have grown up to love the Lord. And why they've all found spouses who love the Lord. And why they've had so many beautiful children of their own that when they all get together to sing "Happy Birthday, Dear Grandpa," I can't even fit them into the dining room any more. God has thrown open the floodgates of heaven, and He's poured out so many blessings that I literally didn't have enough room for them."

But there's still more.

In Matthew 19:30, Jesus says, "Many who are first will be last, and many who are last will be first." From this, we know that someday—maybe someday soon—God is going to turn everything upside down.

About fifteen years ago, I spent my "quiet time" for a few months just reading through the New Testament with a pink highlighter pen in my hand, and I marked every passage that talks about this "Law of Reversals." That little paperback Bible is still on my desk, and especially in the Gospels, nearly every page of it is highlighted somewhere in pink.

In the gospel of Luke, as soon as Mary finds out that she's going to be the mother of the Messiah, she sings a little song: "[God] has brought down rulers from their thrones but has lifted up the humble. He has filled the hungry with good things but has sent the rich away empty" (1:52–53). Everything is going to be turned upside down.

A page or two later, when John the Baptist finds out that the Messiah is coming, he goes out and preaches, "Every valley shall be filled, and every mountain and hill shall be made low, and the crooked shall be made straight, and the rough ways made smooth" (Luke 3:5 NRSV). Everything is going to be turned upside down.

Shortly after that, Jesus himself stands up for the first time in His hometown synagogue, and He reads from the book of Isaiah: "The Spirit of the Lord is upon me, because he has anointed me to preach good news to the poor. He has sent me to proclaim release to the captives and recovery of sight to the blind, to let the oppressed go free, to proclaim the year of the Lord's favor" (Luke 4:18–19 NRSV). Everything is going to be turned upside down.

Again and again, Jesus returns to that same theme: "Blessed are the meek, for they will inherit the earth"

(Matthew 5:5). "Those who find their life will lose it, and those who lose their life for my sake will find it" (Matthew 10:39 NRSV). "All who exalt themselves will be humbled, and all who humble themselves will be exalted" (Matthew 23:12 NRSV). "Blessed are you who hunger now, for you will be satisfied" (Luke 6:21). "Whoever wants to become great among you must be your servant, and whoever wants to be first must be slave of all" (Mark 10:43–44). And the reversal that guarantees all of these other reversals is this: "The Son of Man is to be betrayed into human hands, and they will kill him, and three days after being killed, *he will rise again*" (Mark 9:31 NRSV).

Everything in this world is going to be turned upside down, and the only people who are going to like the change are the ones who've been leading lives of Christian stewardship. Randy Alcorn is looking at this situation from God's perspective when he says, "Someday this upside down world will be turned right side up again, and nothing in all eternity will turn it back. If we are wise, we will spend our brief lives on earth positioning ourselves for the turn."

I happen to be on the board of a little not-for-profit corporation that tries to help an orphanage in Kenya. In one of the contribution envelopes that came into our post office box, there was an uncommonly generous check for the orphanage, and there was also a Formica color chip from a home-improvement store. Somebody had evidently stopped wanting a new kitchen countertop in order to "position herself for the turn." "For it is in giving that we receive," said Saint Francis. "It is in pardoning that we are pardoned, and it is in dying that we are born to eternal life."

And that's where there's even more.

The Bible says, "If our hope in Christ is only for this life, we are more to be pitied than anyone in the world" (1 Corinthians 15:19 NLT). In this verse, the Bible comes right out and admits that Christian stewardship just may not be worth the effort if all we're going to get out of it is some fleeting liberation in "this life," a shot at transcendence, a few happy surprises, and the chance to end up on the top side of some reversals that have been delayed for two thousand years already. If liberation, transcendence, surprises, and implausible reversals are all that's behind Curtain No. 2, then we might as well pick what's behind Curtain No. 1 like everybody else and grab every prize we can on our way to the graveyard.

But in Matthew 6:19–21, Jesus says, "Do not store up for yourselves treasures on earth, where moth and rust destroy, and where thieves break in and steal. But store up for yourselves treasures in heaven, where moth and rust do not destroy, and where thieves do not break in and steal. For where your treasure is, there your heart will be also." This is yet another one of those places where it helps me understand what Jesus *did* say if I think through what He *didn't* say. And in this verse, I see that Jesus does *not* say, "*Don't* store up treasures." In fact, He says exactly the opposite; He says, "*Do* store up treasures." He just wants us to make sure that we're storing them up in a safe place—namely, heaven. And Jesus does *not* say, "Store up *for God* treasures in heaven." He says, "Store up *for yourselves* treasures in heaven." In other words, the benefits of stewardship don't end at the grave, and we can put our treasures now where we want our hearts to be forever.

I have an old green car that's parked out in the street right now. Moths and rust are destroying it while it sits there, and for all I know, thieves are breaking in to steal it. Thirteen years ago, that car cost my wife and me more than anything else we'd ever bought except our house. It's been a very reliable car, but it's been one lousy treasure. From the day that car was built, it was predestined to the scrapyard. Jesus says not to invest any more than we have to in "treasure" like that.

On the other hand, a reporter once asked British financier Moses Montefiore how much he was worth, and Montefiore gave an answer that everybody knew was way too low. The reporter challenged him, "You must have at least ten times that much money." So Montefiore explained, "You didn't ask me how much I have; you asked me how much I'm worth. The things I own could all be wiped out in a minute, but the money I've given away is what measures what I'm really worth." Moses Montefiore didn't realize it, but Jesus would have called that kind of money a "treasure in heaven."

Treasures in heaven have one feature, though, that might make us as indignant about them as we are about steroid abusers getting into the record books. In Luke 23:43, Jesus says to the thief next to Him on the cross, "I tell you the truth, today you will be with me in paradise." Somehow, I don't think that thief had ever been a paragon of stewardship. Is he going to get the same treasure in heaven that I've worked so hard to store up? After all, Ephesians 2:8–9 says, "It is by grace you have been saved, through faith—and this is not from yourselves, it is the gift of God—not by works, so that no one can boast."

But wait one minute. Proverbs 24:12 says, "[God] will repay all people as their actions deserve" (NLT). And Hebrews 10:36 says, "You need to persevere so that *when you have done the will of God*, you will receive what he has promised." And in Matthew 16:27, Jesus promises that "he will reward each person according to what he has done." So here we go again with one more paradox: Ephesians says, "not by works," and the book of Matthew says, "according to what we have done." And how could we possibly embrace both of those statements at the same time?

For such a tough nut, this one is surprisingly easy to crack. Exactly what is it that Ephesians says we'll receive by grace, through faith, and not by works? It's salvation. And exactly what is it that the book of Matthew says we'll receive according to what we have done? That's rewards. In other words, if any of us make it into heaven at all, it'll be as a free gift of God's grace, His undeserved favor. But once we've arrived in heaven by grace through faith, the Bible doesn't hesitate to say that our works will be judged, and our rewards will differ. The Bible describes the situation this way: "On the judgment day, fire will reveal what kind of work each builder has done. The fire will show if a person's work has any value. If the work survives, that builder will receive a reward. But if the work is burned up, the builder will suffer great loss. *The builder will be saved*, but like someone barely escaping through a wall of flames" (1 Corinthians 3:13–15 NLT).

This isn't to say that some people will end up moping around heaven, kicking themselves forever because they didn't store up as much treasure as they could have. The situation will probably be more like what happened to my little sister on our family trip to Washington DC, when we were kids. My sister was still too little to appreciate the historic sites, so even though she had a great time at the Capitol and the White House and the Washington Monument, when we got home, all she could remember about them was their drinking fountains. That could be a little picture of how it will be in heaven. Some of us will be having an absolutely great time in glory, but we'll still be too "little" to appreciate anything but the drinking fountains. Other people who've grown up by practicing stewardship during their lives on earth will have more of a capacity to enjoy paradise. That's one of the reasons the Bible says, "Do you not know that in a race all the runners run, but only one gets the prize? Run in such a way as to get the prize" (1 Corinthians 9:24).

So rewards in heaven are part of the plan of God, even if some of us do keep trying to turn them down. We say, "I'm just a humble servant of the Lord; I don't expect—I don't even want—a reward." But that's wrong. Dead wrong. Saying to God, "I don't want a reward in heaven" is the same as saying, "I don't want anything that I can use for the praise of your glory." After all, if we're planning to join in with the other saints, "casting down our golden crowns around the glassy sea," then exactly where do we think we're going to get those crowns in the first place? And besides, working for heavenly rewards doesn't make us selfish. C. S. Lewis wrote that "Heaven offers nothing a mercenary soul can desire. It is safe to tell the pure in heart that they shall see God, for only the pure in heart would want to. There are rewards that do not sully motives." And the Bible tells us that Jesus himself was motivated by rewards. The writer of Hebrews 12:2 says that it was because of "*the joy set before him*" that Jesus "endured the cross, scorning its shame."

We've gone off on a long tangent here, but to get back to the main point, we saw that Paul wrote, "If our hope in Christ is only for this life, we are more to be pitied than anyone in the world" (1 Corinthians 15:19 NLT). But our hope in Christ *doesn't* cover only this life. "For our light and momentary troubles are achieving for us an eternal glory that far outweighs them all," says the apostle Paul.

"So we fix our eyes not on what is seen, but on what is unseen. For what is seen is temporary, but what is unseen is eternal" (2 Corinthians 4:17–18). When it comes to treasure, it's true that "you can't take it with you"—but you *can* send it on ahead.

And there's still even more.

In Matthew 19:28–29, Jesus says something that jumps off the page like two-inch type. He says, "I tell you the truth, at the renewal of all things, when the Son of Man sits on his glorious throne, . . . everyone who has left houses, or [family] or fields for my sake will receive a hundred times as much and will inherit eternal life." Just read the words: "At the renewal of all things," when we'll hear a loud voice from the throne saying, "Look, God's home is now among his people!" (Revelation 21:3 NLT), then Jesus will reward us with a hundred times as much as anything we've ever passed up for Him. *A hundred times as much*—that's a 10,000 percent return on investment, compounded continuously over the extended period of eternity. Proverbs 19:17 says, "Whoever is kind to the poor lends to the Lord, and will be repaid in full" (NRSV). That must be the understatement of the millennium. When these mortal bodies put on immortality, we will be well fixed, in more ways than one.

And how does an eternity of rewards compare to a lifetime of occasional self-denial? In James Joyce's *A Portrait of the Artist as a Young Man*, a priest in an Irish boys' school tries to explain eternity like this:

You have often seen the sand on the seashore. How fine are its tiny grains! And how many of those tiny little grains go to make up the small handful which a child grasps in its play. Now imagine a mountain of that sand, a million miles high, reaching from the earth to the farthest heavens, and a million miles broad, extending to remotest space, and a million miles in thickness; and imagine such an enormous mass of countless particles of sand multiplied as often as there are leaves in the forest, drops of water in the mighty ocean, feathers on birds, scales on fish, hairs on animals, . . . and imagine that at the end of every million years a little bird came to that mountain and carried away in its beak a tiny grain of that sand . . . How many eons upon eons of ages before it had carried away all? . . . And if that mountain rose again after it had been all carried away, and if the bird came again and carried it all away again grain by grain, and if it so rose and sank as many times as there are stars in the sky . . . leaves on the trees, feathers upon birds, scales upon fish, hairs upon animals, at the end of all those innumerable risings and sinkings of that immeasurably vast mountain *not one single instant of eternity could be said to have ended* . . . Eternity would scarcely have begun.

This is what we're playing with so casually: *eternity*. Every whisper of our credit cards going through the swiper at the drug store will echo across heaven for eternity. And not just across heaven but also across the Holy City, the New Jerusalem that the Bible promises will be "coming down out of heaven from God, prepared as a bride adorned for her husband." And at that time, it will be only those "who overcome" who will "inherit all things" (Revelation 21:2, 7 NKJV).

We remember the missionary-martyr Jim Elliot for his one big line, "He is no fool who gives up what he cannot keep in order to gain what he cannot lose." But God isn't even asking us to give up what we can't keep; he's just inviting us to move it to safer places—places that Jesus describes in Luke 12:33 as "purses . . . that will not wear out, a treasure in heaven that will not be exhausted."

Along our way to that eternal reward, the Bible says that there'll be "a time to plant and a time to uproot . . . , a time to tear down and a time to build . . . , a time to keep and a time to throw away" (Ecclesiastes 3:2, 3, 6). There'll be a time to save and a time to spend. A time to give and a time to receive. A time to borrow and a time to lend. A time to feast and a time to fast.

One person who recognized a time to spend when she saw it was that nameless woman in Mark 14 who gave Jesus a jar of expensive lotion. From what little we know about this woman, she couldn't have been wealthy, and she must have had to scrimp and save in order to honor Jesus with such a lavish gift. I've always felt a little bit embarrassed for her, though, because right in the middle of her fifteen minutes of fame, she fumbled her alabaster jar of lotion, and it broke. Why did the gospel writers have to put that right into the Bible—a perpetual record of her clumsy little accident? Unless maybe it wasn't an accident. Unless maybe this woman *purposely* broke the jar as a way of saying to Jesus, "I don't need a jar to take anything home in; I've given it all to you."

When we consider the wild immoderation of God's love for us in Jesus Christ, our only reasonable response is reckless abandon to His kingdom. And so, if there can be a patron saint of Christian stewardship, I nominate this woman who poured out all she had for Jesus and then smashed the jar in a flamboyant gesture of holding nothing back.

> *Worthy is the Lamb, who was slain,*
> *to receive power and wealth*
> *and wisdom and strength*
> *and honor and glory and praise.*
> *(Revelation 5:12)*

LOOSE CHANGE

"Dunghill mists away may fly"

The prospect of eternal rewards gives us a way of dealing with loss, and nobody has ever expressed this more poignantly than Anne Bradstreet, the wife of the governor of Massachusetts during the colonial period. In the middle of a summer night, somebody woke up the

Bradstreet family with "the fearful sound of 'Fire!' and
'Fire!'" And Mrs. Bradstreet had to stand outside in her
nightgown and watch everything she had ever owned go
up in flames. She wrote,

> *And when I could no longer look,*
> *I blest His name who gave and took.*

Of course, knowing that everything belongs to God
didn't make it easy for Anne Bradstreet to deal with the
loss of everything that God had ever entrusted to her.

> *When by the ruins oft I passed*
> *My sorrowing eyes aside did cast.*
> *Here stood that trunk, and there that chest.*
> *There lay the store I counted best.*
> *My pleasant things in ashes lie,*
> *And them behold no more shall I.*

It must have taken months—probably years—but
when Anne Bradstreet had appropriately grieved her loss,
she began repeating to herself the truths about God's
ownership. And in her poem, she says that her grief over
her possessions started to seem about as important as the
steam from a manure pile on a frosty morning.

> *Then I began my heart to chide:*
> *And did thy wealth on earth abide?*
> *Didst fix thy hope on moldering dust?*
> *The arm of flesh didst make thy trust?*

Raise up thy thoughts above the sky
That dunghill mists away may fly.
Thou hast a house on high erect,
Framed by that mighty Architect.
The world no longer let me love,
My hope and treasure lie above.

The rest of this poem can be found in nearly any American Literature anthology under some variation of the title "Verses Upon the Burning of Our House, July 10th, 1666."

Ignore these guidelines

We've spent a lot of time documenting a set of guidelines that can help us live in the dynamic tensions among all of the Bible's paradoxical statements about money. But now we would be wise not to follow these guidelines too religiously. We don't want stewardship itself to become the god of our idolatry. When we partner with God to live within the guidelines of stewardship, success doesn't come from following the guidelines, but from following the Partner.

NEGOTIABLES

"Content to let the world go by, to know no gain nor loss"

Financial counselors tell us that high-income investments have high risks, and low-risk investments produce low income. Most of us try to find a comfortable balance somewhere between the extremes of high-income ventures like speculating in rare baseball cards and low-risk alternatives like buying certificates of deposit in a bank. Consider a real example of this. My church has an endowment fund to make sure that we can continue our inner-city ministry even if our inner-city congregation can't always keep up with the bills. We've found a comfortable balance between risks and income by investing the endowment fund very conservatively in the stock market. However, in spite of every precaution, in a market "correction" a few years ago, our fund lost more than a hundred thousand dollars in a single day.

Evaluate this situation from the perspective of the eternal kingdom of God. Instead of our stock market arrangement, what unorthodox kinds of "investments" might seem more risky to the world but would be less risky in the kingdom? What kinds of investments might seem less profitable to the world but could be fantastically profitable for eternity? How willing are we to submit our personal finances to the insights that we can gain from this thought experiment?

Stewardship in reverse

Some churches have experimented with an idea that they call "reverse stewardship." The church passes around an offering plate full of cash, and the members are supposed to take money *out* of the plate and invest it somehow for God, and then return the proceeds to the church by some deadline a few months in the future. For example, somebody might use the money to buy yarn and knit a sweater, and then sell the sweater and give the proceeds back to the church. Is "reverse stewardship" an accurate name for this exercise? In what ways does this exercise reinforce what we know about stewardship? Are there any ways in which this exercise might undermine people's understanding of biblical stewardship? Overall, is "reverse stewardship" a worthy exercise for a Christian congregation?

A PRAYER OF REPENTANCE

O Lord, when I consider the heavens and the earth, the work of your hands, I understand why you are called Providence . . .

> *But when I catalog my blessings, I am confronted with my own unworthiness.*

Faithful Provider, by whose undeserved favor I enjoy all the benefits of peace, progress, and prosperity . . .

> *Forgive me, that in my greed for even more, I have taken for granted the abundance that I already have.*

Benevolent Spirit, source of all skill and science, all artistry and aptitude, all industry and intellect . . .

> *Forgive me for devoting my giftedness to self-serving enterprises, and leaving your children unfed, unclothed, unwelcomed, and unvisited.*

Eternal Master, by whose inventive power time itself is created . . .

> *Forgive me for squandering in unfruitfulness the hours and days that you have allotted to me.*

Majestic Sustainer, at whose command every particle of the cosmos is recreated at every instant . . .

Forgive me for coveting and hoarding as if your resources might be exhausted before they extend to me.

Sovereign Lord, who blesses me by withholding what I foolishly desire . . .

Forgive me for failing to thank you when the answer to my prayers has been your loving No.

Refining Fire, who uses for good what the world has meant for evil, and who thereby trains me in self-knowledge, and in compassion, and in attentiveness to your still small voice . . .

Forgive my impatience with your tender discipline.

Almighty Protector, who so often spares me from the calamities of this fallen world . . .

Forgive me for neglecting to thank you when nothing at all has happened.

Bountiful Creator of every good and perfect gift, all that you provide becomes contaminated by my iniquity. I have nothing to return to you but sin that needs to be forgiven.

But I look to you in trust for That Day when you will present me faultless before the presence of your glory, with exceeding joy, through the righteousness of Jesus Christ, whom I acknowledge as my Savior, and serve as my Lord. Amen.

A HYMN OF COMMITMENT

Bring a gift in proportion to the way
the Lord your God has blessed you.
— Deuteronomy 16:17

O Jesus, I now promise to give as You shall bless.
Transform my life to echo the vows my lips profess.
Your bounty swells around me; Your precepts are my guide.
May I be open-handed, and You be glorified!

O Jesus, I acknowledge that all I count as mine
Has flowed to us, the branches, from You, the gracious Vine.
I pledge to hold more loosely the things I cannot keep,
In faith that as I scatter, so shall I also reap.

O Jesus, You have promised, to those who freely share,
A hundred-fold repayment, and Your eternal care.
And Jesus, I now promise to give as You shall bless.
Reward in life eternal the vows my lips profess.

These words can be sung to any of the many hymn
tunes that have what is called the 7.6.7.6.D. meter. Some
examples would be the stately tune Aurelia ("The Church's

One Foundation"), or the more militant tune Lancashire ("Lead On O King Eternal"), or the more reflective tune Munich ("O Word of God Incarnate").

RESOURCES
FOR FURTHER STUDY

MONEY, POSSESSIONS, AND ETERNITY

By Randy C. Alcorn
Tyndale House Publishers, 1989
ISBN-10: 0-84235-360-7   ISBN-13: 978-0-84235-360-1

This is unquestionably the most profound, the most challenging, and the most thoroughly biblical 450-page book ever written about the cosmic significance and the eternal consequences of what we do with money and possessions.

FINANCIAL PEACE: RESTORING FINANCIAL HOPE TO YOU AND YOUR FAMILY

By Dave Ramsey
Viking Press, 1997
ISBN-10: 0-67087-361-6   ISBN-13: 978-0-67087-361-6

This is the most readable and practical book available on the nuts and bolts of managing a household budget, getting out of debt, and saving for the future. It's not at all a theological book, but its suggestions do grow out of a solidly biblical value system.

GENEROUS PEOPLE: HOW TO ENCOURAGE VITAL STEWARDSHIP

By Eugene Grimm
Abington Press, 1992
ISBN-10: 0-68714-045-5   ISBN-13: 978-0-68714-045-9

This may be the only book in existence that approaches fundraising in the church as a Christ-centered opportunity for spiritual growth rather than as a Madison Avenue gimmick for wringing more money out of people.

FREEDOM OF SIMPLICITY

By Richard Foster
Harper, 2005 (latest edition)
ISBN-10: 0-06075-971-2   ISBN-13: 978-0-06075-971-1

Richard Foster finds that simplicity is not just for communes and monasteries but also for work-a-day people who long for a Spirit-filled liberation from the tyranny of money, possessions, and keeping up with the Joneses.

RICH CHRISTIANS IN AN AGE OF HUNGER

By Ronald J. Sider
Thomas Nelson, 2005 (latest edition)
ISBN-10: 0-84994-530-5   ISBN-13: 978-0-84994-530-4

The cover of one edition of this book notes that when it was first published, it caused "turmoil" in the Christian community with its unflinching look at how our great blessings can't be separated from our great responsibilities.